I0606282

Early
ANIMAL
Encyclopedias

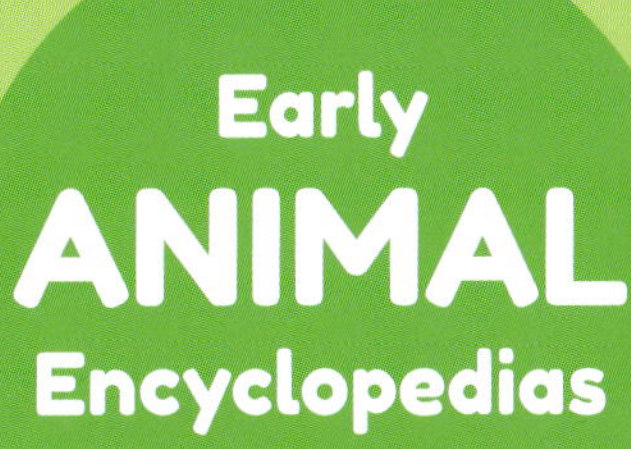

DINOSAURS

by Kathryn Hulick

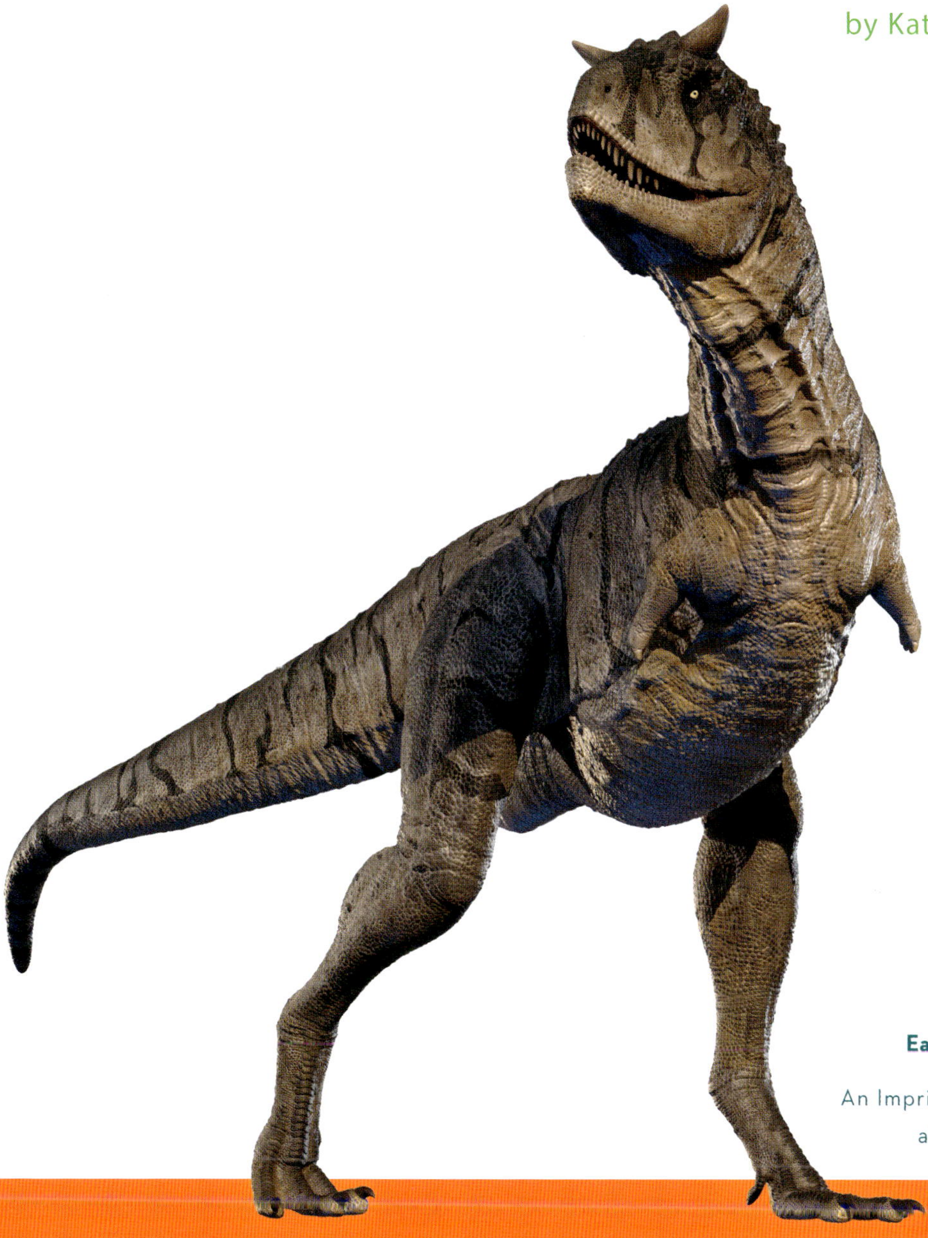

Early Encyclopedias

An Imprint of Abdo Reference
abdobooks.com

abdobooks.com

Published by Abdo Reference, a division of ABDO, PO Box 398166, Minneapolis, Minnesota 55439.

Printed in China
102022
012023

THIS BOOK CONTAINS RECYCLED MATERIALS

Editor: Katharine Hale
Series Designers: Candice Keimig, Joshua Olson

Library of Congress Control Number: 2022940667

Publisher's Cataloging-in-Publication Data

Names: Hulick, Kathryn, author.
Title: Dinosaurs / by Kathryn Hulick
Description: Minneapolis, Minnesota: Abdo Publishing, 2023 | Series: Early animal encyclopedias | Includes online resources and index.
Identifiers: ISBN 9781098290405 (lib. bdg.) | ISBN 9781098275723 (ebook)
Subjects: LCSH: Dinosaurs--Juvenile literature. | Dinosaurs--Behavior--Juvenile literature. | Zoology--Juvenile literature. | Encyclopedias and dictionaries--Juvenile literature.
Classification: DDC 567.903--dc23

CONTENTS

Dinosaurs roamed Earth for many millions of years.

The World of Dinosaurs

Millions of years ago, dinosaurs stomped, dashed, and glided around Earth. Many grew to incredible sizes. Others were very small. Some hunted and ate meat. Others grazed on plants. All dinosaurs were reptiles.

Dinosaurs evolved and went extinct, or died out, during three time periods. The first is the Triassic. This period began 252 million years ago. Back then, Earth was much warmer than it is today. The continents were one landmass. It was called Pangaea (pan-JEE-uh). The Jurassic Period was 201 million to 145 million years ago. The Cretaceous came last. The continents slowly separated during these time periods. An asteroid hit Earth 66 million years ago. This ended the Cretaceous Period. Most dinosaurs went extinct. But some survived. They continued to evolve. Birds are the living descendants of dinosaurs.

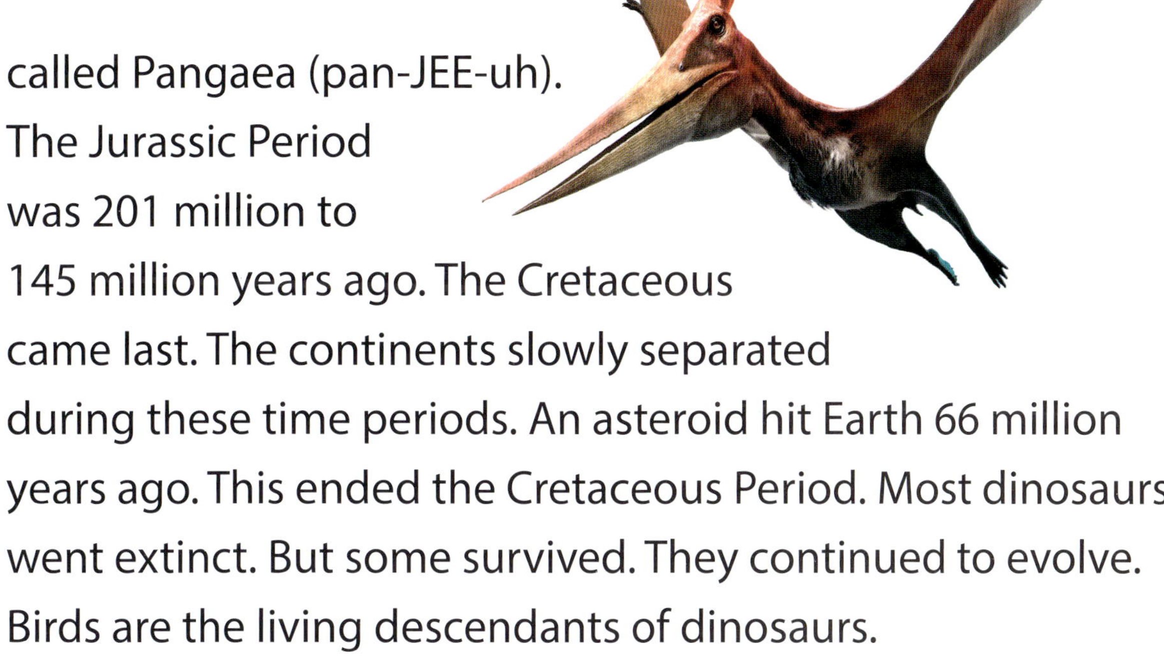

Sometimes dinosaur bones, footprints, eggs, and other remains got preserved. These are called fossils. Scientists use fossils to learn more about dinosaurs.

Pterosaurs, *above*, and plesiosaurs, *below*, were not dinosaurs. But they lived at the same time as dinosaurs.

ALLOSAURUS

(a-luh-SOHR-uhs)

Range

Allosaurus was a top predator during the Late Jurassic Period. It is part of a group of meat-eating dinosaurs called theropods. *Allosaurus* was very common in what is now North America. Fossils that may be from *Allosaurus* have also been found in Portugal, Tanzania, Siberia, and Australia.

Appearance

Allosaurus could grow bigger than a school bus. It looked like *Tyrannosaurus*. But it was slightly smaller. *Allosaurus* also had longer arms and small horns over its eyes. It had sharp claws and long, sharp teeth with serrated edges.

Allosaurus fossil

Ferocious Predator

Allosaurus could run very fast. It ate plant-eaters, including *Camarasaurus* and *Stegosaurus*. Most likely, it hunted alone. It may also have been a scavenger. This means it ate creatures that had recently died.

Length:
39 to 43 feet
(12 to 13 m)

Weight:
2.2 tons
(2 metric tons)

When Did This Dinosaur Live?

AMARGASAURUS

(uh-MAHR-guh-SOHR-uhs)

Range

Amargasaurus lived during the Early Cretaceous Period. It roamed in the forests of what is now South America. Only one fossil of this dinosaur has ever been found.

Appearance

This plant-eater had two rows of long spines along its neck. It was smaller than most of its sauropod cousins. Its neck was shorter too. But it was still a huge animal.

Length:
39 feet
(12 m)

Weight:
9.9 tons
(9 metric tons)

When Did This Dinosaur Live?

Triassic Period	Jurassic Period	Cretaceous Period	
252 million years ago	201 million years ago	145 million years ago	66 million years ago

Amargasaurus fossil

Mysterious Spines

Amargasaurus's spines puzzle dinosaur scientists. They do not know what exactly the spines did. The spines may have held up flaps of skin that looked like sails. Or perhaps the dinosaur rattled the spines to make noise. The sails or spines could have helped attract mates. Or maybe they scared away predators.

ANCHIORNIS

(an-kee-OHR-nihs)

Tiny Dino

Anchiornis was first discovered in China in 2009. This dinosaur lived during the Late Jurassic Period. It is one of the smallest, lightest dinosaurs ever found.

Appearance

Length:
1.3 feet
(0.4 m)

Weight:
8.8 ounces
(250 g)

Anchiornis was the same size as a chicken and had feathers. But unlike a chicken, *Anchiornis* had four wings. Feathers sprouted from both its arms and legs. In *Anchiornis* fossils, these feathers have lost their original colors. But scientists studied them carefully. They took samples from a fossil. They compared the samples to modern birds. The scientists were able to figure out the color of the dinosaur. *Anchiornis* was black and white with a red crest.

***Anchiornis* fossil**

Climbing and Gliding

Most likely, *Anchiornis* could not fly. It probably climbed trees with its claws and glided around. It hunted lizards, fish, and other small animals.

When Did This Dinosaur Live?

Triassic Period	Jurassic Period	Cretaceous Period

252 million years ago — 201 million years ago — 145 million years ago — 66 million years ago

ANKYLOSAURUS

(an-KEYE-loh-SOHR-uhs)

Range

Ankylosaurus lived in what is now the United States. This plant-eater lived in the Late Cretaceous Period. It went extinct after an asteroid struck Earth. All the large dinosaurs living at this time also died out.

Length: 33 feet (10 m)

Weight: 4.4 tons (4 metric tons)

Appearance

Spikes and hard plates protected *Ankylosaurus.* Its tail ended in a huge, bony club. It had short legs and a short neck. *Ankylosaurus* grew up

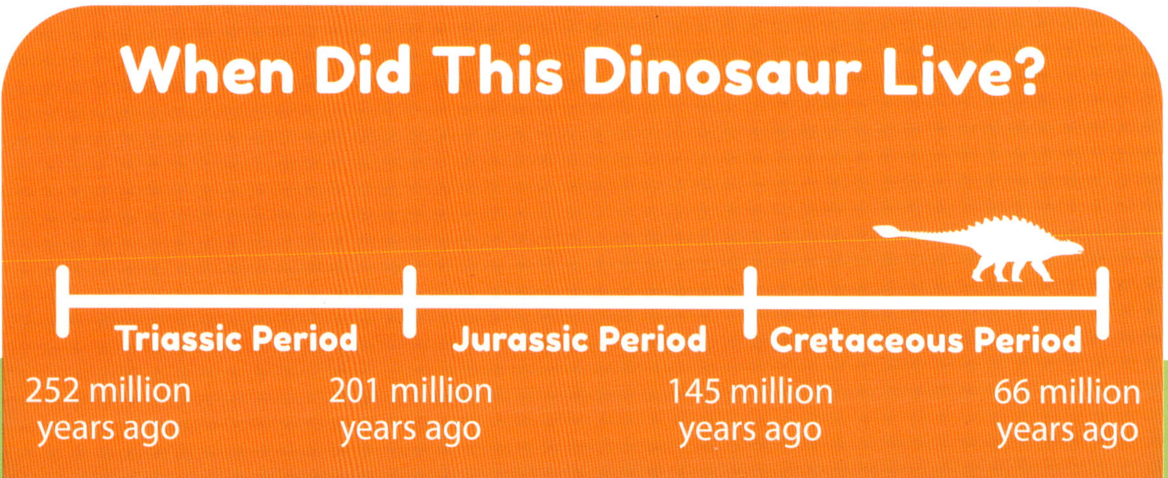

Ankylosaurus fossil

to 33 feet (10 m) long. It weighed as much as 4.4 tons (4 metric tons). It was the largest of a family of armored dinosaurs called ankylosaurs.

Ready for Battle

Ankylosaurus was too slow and heavy to run from a fight. It used its powerful armor for protection. Its enemies included *Tyrannosaurus*. It likely swung its tail to defend itself.

APATOSAURUS

(uh-PAT-uh-SOHR-uhs)

Range

Apatosaurus was a huge, plant-eating dinosaur. It lived during the Late Jurassic Period. Its fossils have been found in the United States.

Appearance

Apatosaurus was a sauropod. Like most sauropods, it had a long neck, a small head, and a long tail. *Apatosaurus* grew up to 69 feet (21 m) long. It weighed as much as 33 tons (30 metric tons).

When Did This Dinosaur Live?

Triassic Period | Jurassic Period | Cretaceous Period

252 million years ago | 201 million years ago | 145 million years ago | 66 million years ago

Apatosaurus fossil

The *Brontosaurus* Mix-Up

In the 1870s, *Apatosaurus* and its cousin *Brontosaurus* were discovered. In 1903, scientists decided they were actually the same dinosaur. Then researchers carefully studied almost 100 fossils of each dinosaur. In 2015, they published what they found. *Brontosaurus* was different enough to deserve its own name. *Apatosaurus* was bigger and had a thicker neck.

Length:
69 feet
(21 m)

Weight:
33 tons
(30 metric tons)

ARCHAEOPTERYX

(ahr-kee-AHP-ter-ihks)

Dinosaur or Bird?

Archaeopteryx used to be called the first bird. It was actually both a dinosaur and a bird. It links the dinosaurs of the past to the birds of today. Its name means "ancient wing." It lived during the Late Jurassic Period in what is now Germany. Some fossils are very well preserved. They show this dinosaur's feathers.

Length: 2 feet (0.6 m)

Weight: Around 2 pounds (0.9 kg)

Appearance

Archaeopteryx was the size of a raven. It had two wings and

When Did This Dinosaur Live?

Triassic Period	Jurassic Period	Cretaceous Period

252 million years ago — 201 million years ago — 145 million years ago — 66 million years ago

a beak. Unlike modern birds, it had teeth in its beak. It also had a long, bony tail covered with feathers.

Archaeopteryx fossil

Ready for Takeoff

Archaeopteryx could probably fly. But scientists do not think it was a very strong or graceful flier. It likely climbed, glided, hopped, and flew in short bursts. It hunted insects and small animals.

ARGENTINOSAURUS

(ahr-juhn-TEE-nuh-SOHR-uhs)

Range

Argentinosaurus got its name because its fossils were found in Argentina. It was a massive plant-eater. *Argentinosaurus* lived during the middle of the Cretaceous Period.

Appearance

Argentinosaurus probably grew as long as three school buses and weighed as much as five fire trucks! Scientists think it stretched its long neck to eat leaves from tall trees. No skull has been found. This means scientists do not know what its head looked like.

Length:
115 to 131 feet
(35 to 40 m)

Weight:
Up to 110 tons
(100 metric tons)

The Biggest Ever?

Argentinosaurus belongs to a group of dinosaurs

The scientists who discovered *Argentinosaurus* pose with some of its bones.

called titanosaurs. The word *titan* means "giant." These were the largest animals to ever live on Earth. *Argentinosaurus* may have been the biggest of them all. But only a few fossils have been found. Scientists can only guess this dinosaur's full size.

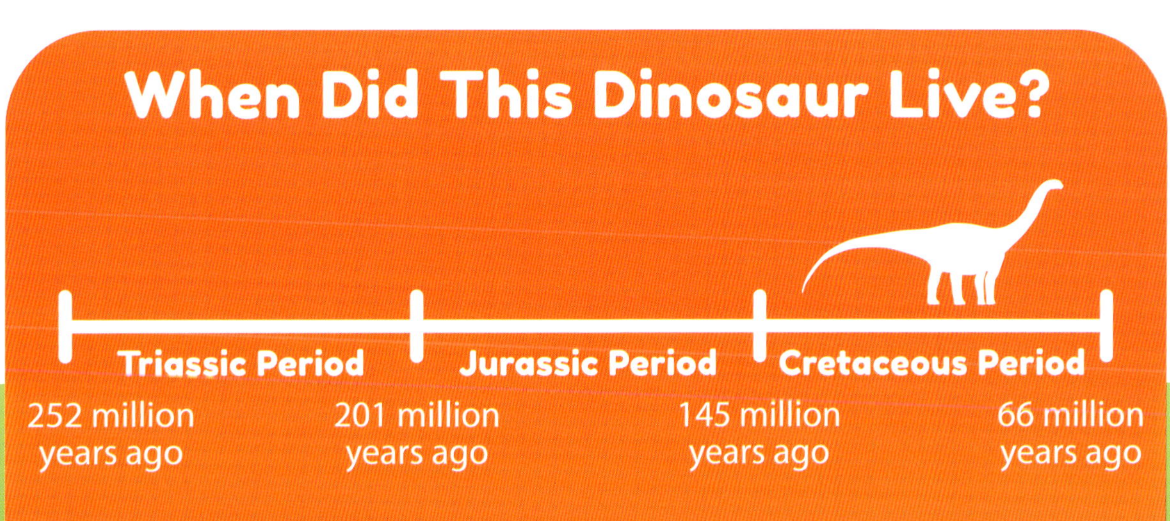

BARYONYX

(beh-ree-AHN-ihks)

Range

Baryonyx lived in what is now England during the Early Cretaceous Period. It likely hunted along riverbanks. Sometimes *Baryonyx* waded into the water. Scientists found the remains of a last meal along with a *Baryonyx* fossil. It had eaten fish and other dinosaurs.

Length:
33 feet
(10 m)

Weight:
2.2 tons
(2 metric tons)

Appearance

Baryonyx had a head similar to a crocodile's. It grabbed fish in its long jaws, which were filled with sharp teeth. But it was twice the size of the largest crocodile. And it walked on two legs. It also may have speared fish with large, curved claws on its hands.

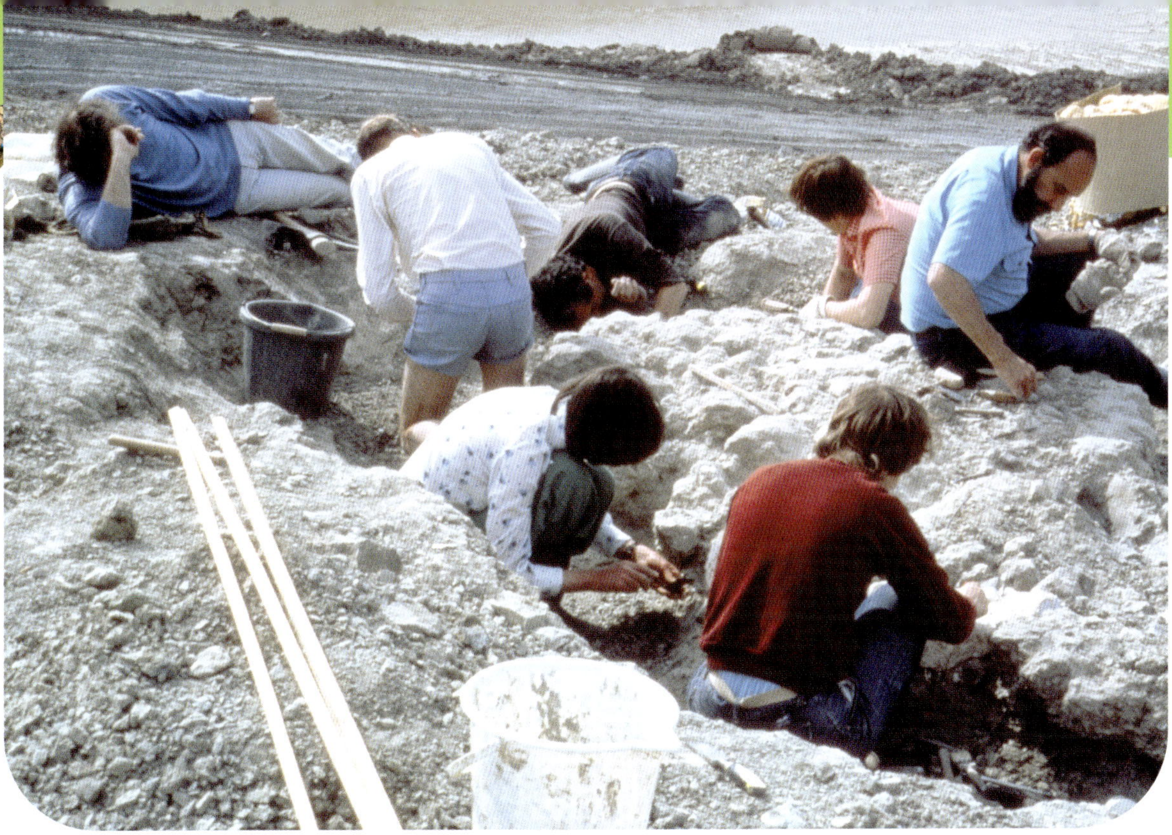

Scientists dig up a *Baryonyx* fossil in England.

A Lucky Find

Baryonyx was discovered in 1983. A plumber who liked to hunt fossils found a huge claw. It was 1 foot (30 cm) long! That led to the name *Baryonyx*, which means "heavy claw."

When Did This Dinosaur Live?

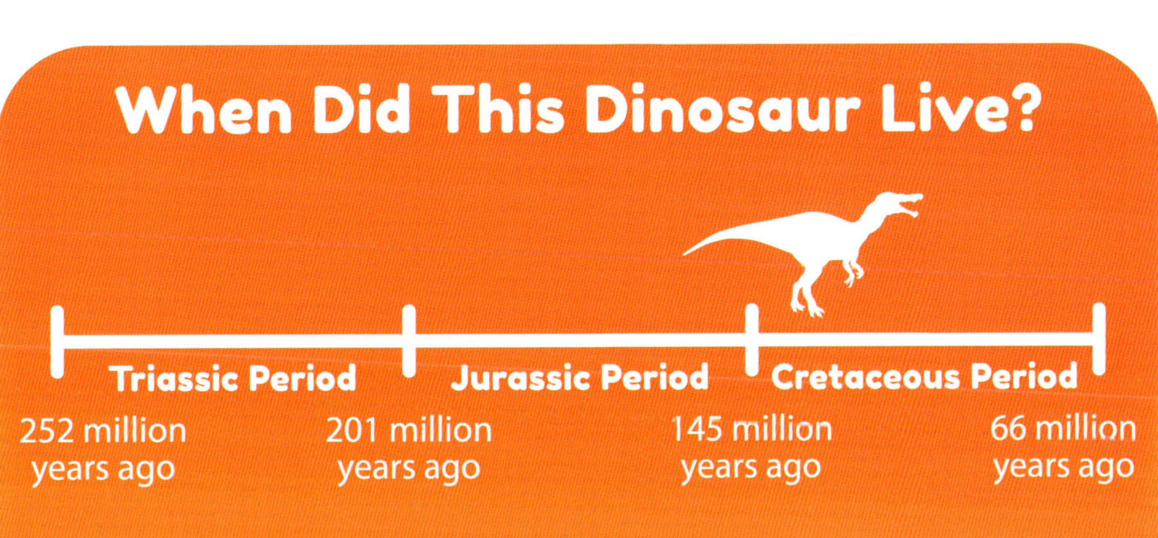

BRACHIOSAURUS

(BRAK-ee-uh-SOHR-uhs)

Length:
82 feet
(25 m)

Weight:
88 tons
(80 metric tons)

Range

Brachiosaurus lived in what is now the United States. It was around during the Late Jurassic Period. The first *Brachiosaurus* fossils were found in 1900.

Appearance

Like other sauropods, *Brachiosaurus* had a very long neck and a small head. Its front legs were longer than its back legs. As a result, its

When Did This Dinosaur Live?

Triassic Period | Jurassic Period | Cretaceous Period

252 million years ago | 201 million years ago | 145 million years ago | 66 million years ago

A *Brachiosaurus* sculpture stands outside the Field Museum in Chicago, Illinois.

back sloped downward. *Brachiosaurus* means "arm reptile."

Taller Than a House

Brachiosaurus was a massive creature that weighed up to 88 tons (80 metric tons). It was one of the tallest dinosaurs, growing almost twice as tall as a two-story house! Thanks to its long front legs and even longer neck, *Brachiosaurus* could reach leaves at the tops of tall trees. It likely swallowed its food whole.

CAMARASAURUS

(KA-muh-ruh-SOHR-uhs)

Range

Camarasaurus roamed what is now the United States. It lived during the Late Jurassic Period. It was one of the most common dinosaurs during this time.

Appearance

Camarasaurus was a medium-sized sauropod. But it was still a large animal. It grew up to 59 feet (18 m) long and weighed around 22 tons (20 metric tons). It had long teeth shaped like spoons. It likely ate tough plants such as ferns. It had huge nostrils near the top of its head. This means it may have had a trunk like an elephant.

Camarasaurus fossil

Strength in Numbers

Camarasaurus likely traveled in large groups called herds. Being in a group may have helped protect them from predators. *Allosaurus* may have been one of *Camarasaurus*'s predators.

Length:
59 feet
(18 m)

Weight: 
22 tons
(20 metric tons)

When Did This Dinosaur Live?

Triassic Period | Jurassic Period | Cretaceous Period

252 million years ago | 201 million years ago | 145 million years ago | 66 million years ago

CARCHARODONTOSAURUS

(kahr-KEH-ruh-dahn-tuh-SOHR-uhs)

When *Carcharodontosaurus, right*, roamed Earth, the Sahara Desert had lots of water.

Range

Carcharodontosaurus was alive during the Cretaceous Period. It lived in what is now the Sahara Desert in Africa. But back then, this region was filled with rivers and plants.

Appearance

Carcharodontosaurus was a deadly meat-eater. *Tyrannosaurus* is a more famous dinosaur.

But *Carcharodontosaurus* was bigger. It had triangular, serrated teeth. Its name means "shark-toothed reptile."

Length:
46 to 49 feet
(14 to 15 m)

Weight:
7.7 to 8.8 tons
(7 to 8 metric tons)

Fighting for Territory

Large, meat-eating dinosaurs needed a lot of space for hunting. Each *Carcharodontosaurus* may have ruled over a patch of land roughly the size of Chicago, Illinois. They likely fought each other for territory.

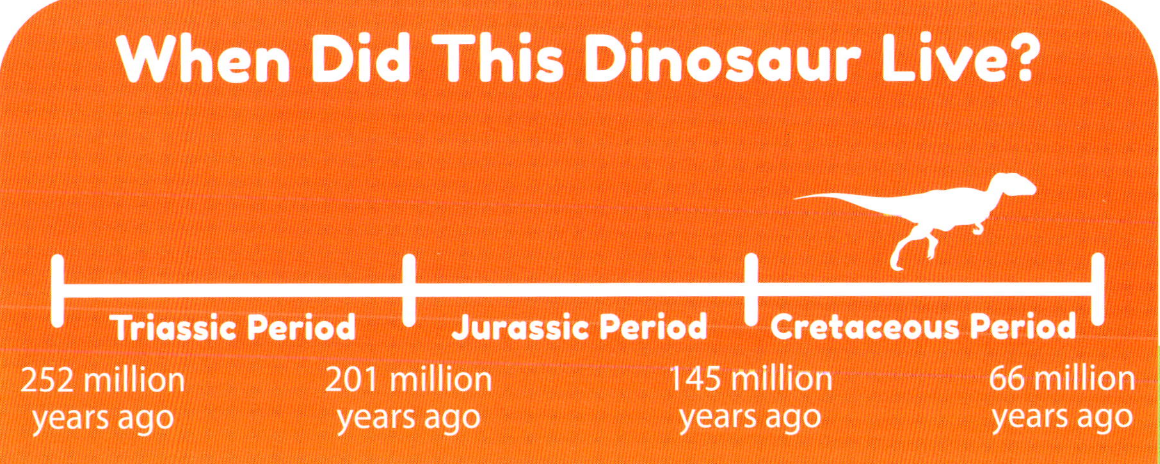

CARNOTAURUS

(kahr-nuh-TOHR-uhs)

Range

The name *Carnotaurus* means "meat-eating bull." During the Late Cretaceous Period, *Carnotaurus* lived in what is now Argentina. It hunted other dinosaurs.

Appearance

Carnotaurus was a deadly but odd-looking dinosaur. Two horns grew over its eyes. They could be 6 inches (15 cm) long. *Carnotaurus* had very short jaws. Its small, stubby arms likely had no purpose. It was a bit shorter than a school bus at 25 feet (7.6 m) long. Scientists have found patches of its skin. It was scaly like a lizard's.

Length:
25 feet
(7.6 m)

Weight:
1.1 tons
(1 metric ton)

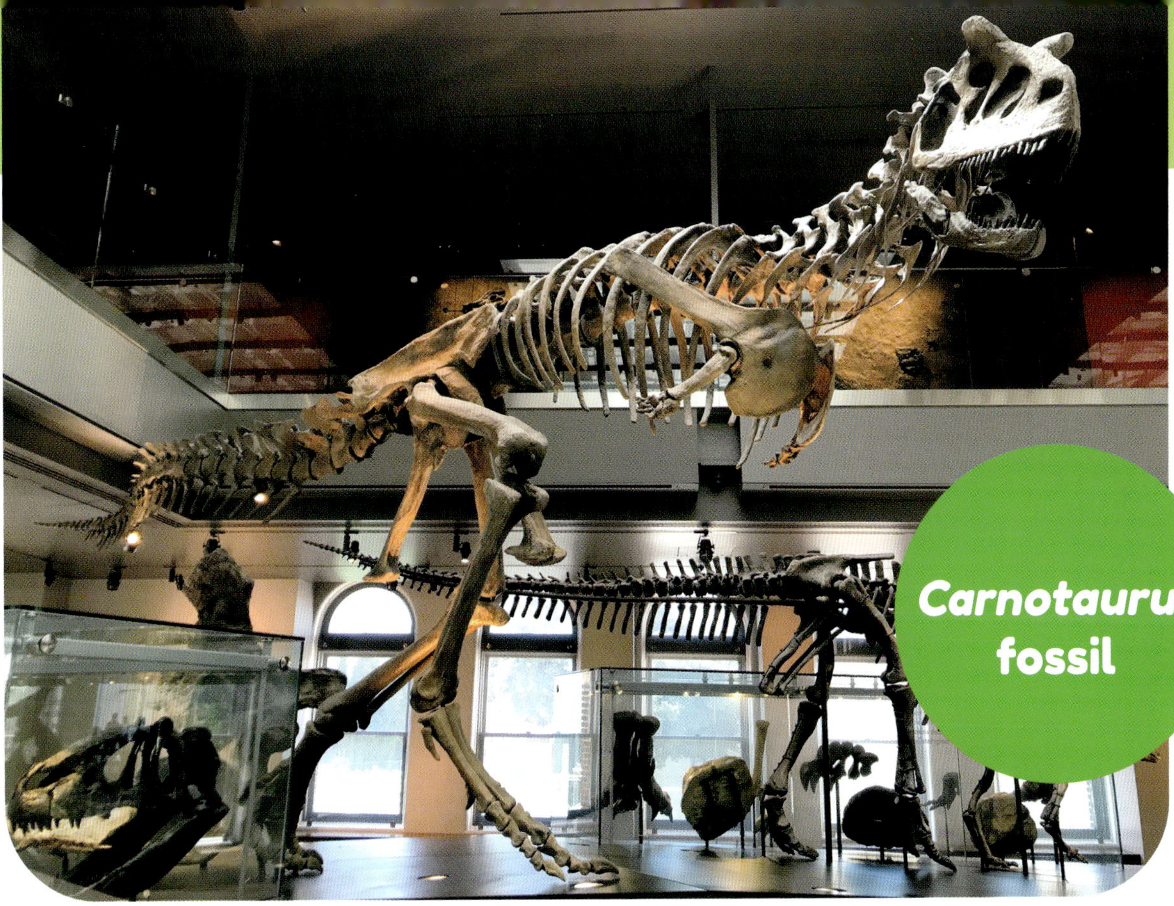

Carnotaurus fossil

Speedy Hunter

Scientists think that *Carnotaurus* could run at speeds of 35 miles per hour (56 kmh). That is as fast as a leopard. It was probably the speediest of all large theropods.

When Did This Dinosaur Live?

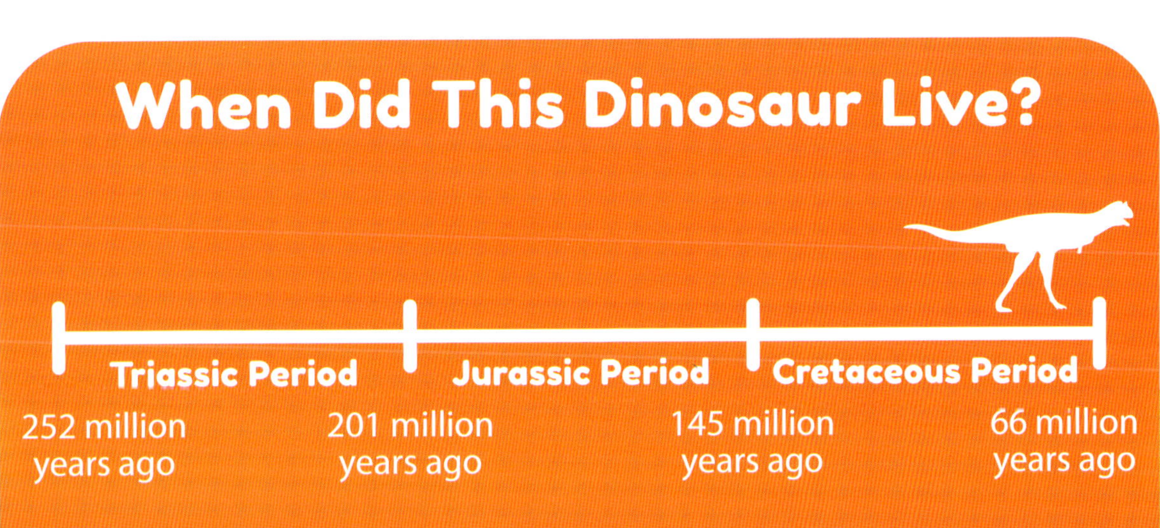

CERATOSAURUS

(ser-AT-uh-SOHR-uhs)

Range

Ceratosaurus lived during the Late Jurassic Period. It was a meat-eater. *Ceratosaurus* fossils have been found in North America, Europe, and Africa.

Appearance

Ceratosaurus was a medium-sized theropod. Still, it weighed more than even the largest bear alive today. *Ceratosaurus* was 20 feet (6 m) long. It had long, sharp fangs that likely stuck out even when its mouth was closed. Bony plates ran down

Ceratosaurus fossil

its back. Horns over its nose and eyes made it look like a dragon.

Count Those Fingers

Theropods ran on two powerful legs. They evolved to use their arms less and less. Later theropods had very stubby arms with just two or three fingers. *Ceratosaurus* was an early theropod. Its short arms still had four fingers.

Length:
20 feet
(6 m)

Weight: 
1 ton
(0.9 metric tons)

COELOPHYSIS

(see-loh-FEYE-sihs)

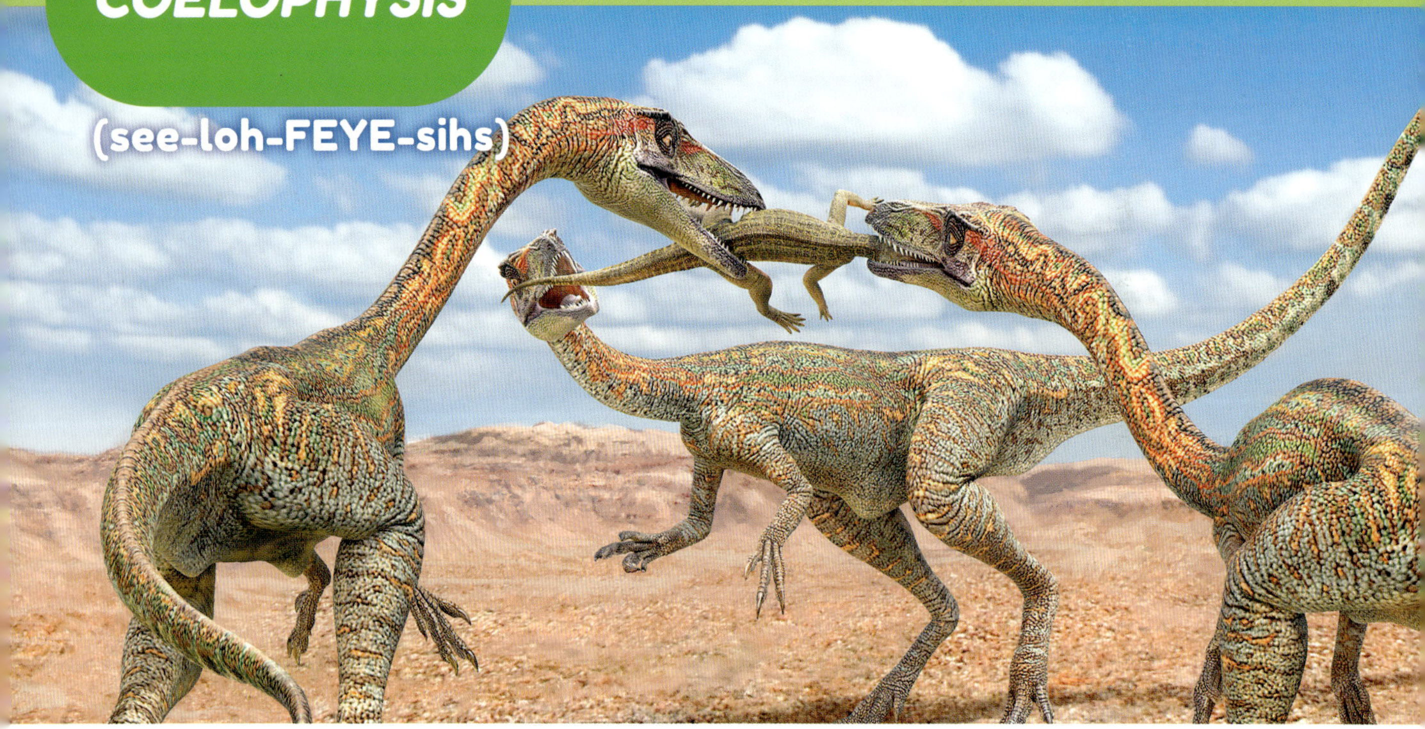

Early Dinosaur

Coelophysis lived around 200 million years ago. This was during the Late Triassic Period. It was one of the earliest dinosaurs. It was a

Length:
9.8 feet
(3 m)

Weight:
51 pounds
(23 kg)

When Did This Dinosaur Live?

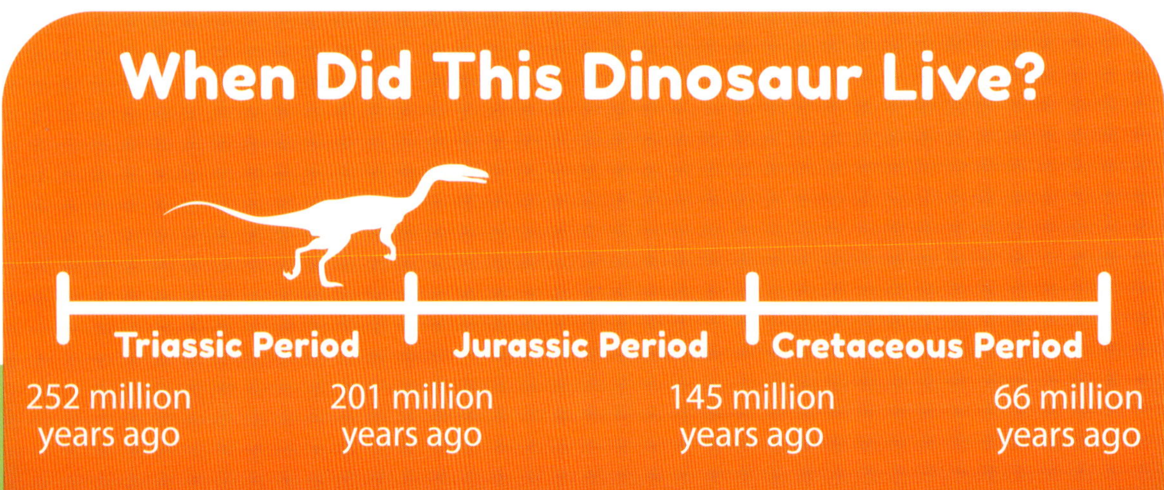

meat-eater that hunted small animals. Its fossils have been found in North America and southern Africa.

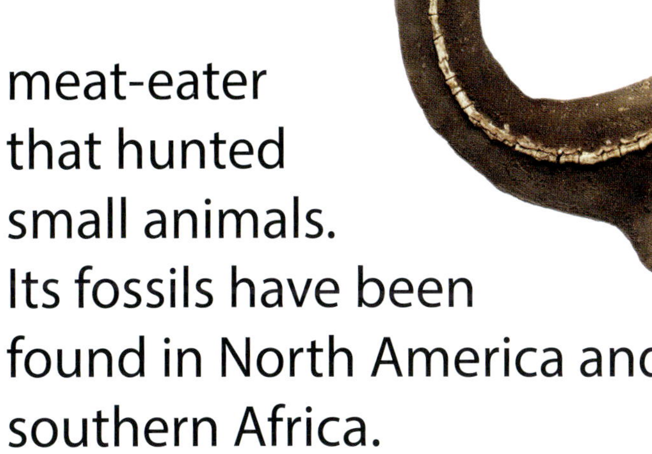

Coelophysis fossil

Appearance

Coelophysis was small, light, and quick. It ran on its two back legs and had small arms. It grew up to 9.8 feet (3 m) long. It was around the same size as an ostrich. However, it weighed less than half as much.

State Fossil

In 1947, thousands of *Coelophysis* fossils were discovered all together at one site in New Mexico. They may have died in a flash flood. *Coelophysis* is now the state fossil of New Mexico.

COMPSOGNATHUS

(kahmp-sahg-NAY-thus)

Range

Compsognathus was a tiny theropod. It was around during the Late Jurassic Period. It lived in what is now Europe.

Length:
3 feet
(0.9 m)

Weight:
12 pounds
(5.5 kg)

Appearance

This dinosaur was about the same size as a house cat. It had hollow bones and a long neck and tail.

Its thin legs ended in long feet. It had three fingers on each hand.

Compsognathus fossil

Built for Speed

Compsognathus was a speedy dinosaur. It likely dashed and darted to hunt small animals and to escape predators. Scientists think it could run at speeds of up to 40 miles per hour (64 kmh). That is twice as fast as a human sprinter can run. It also beats an ostrich, the fastest two-legged animal alive today.

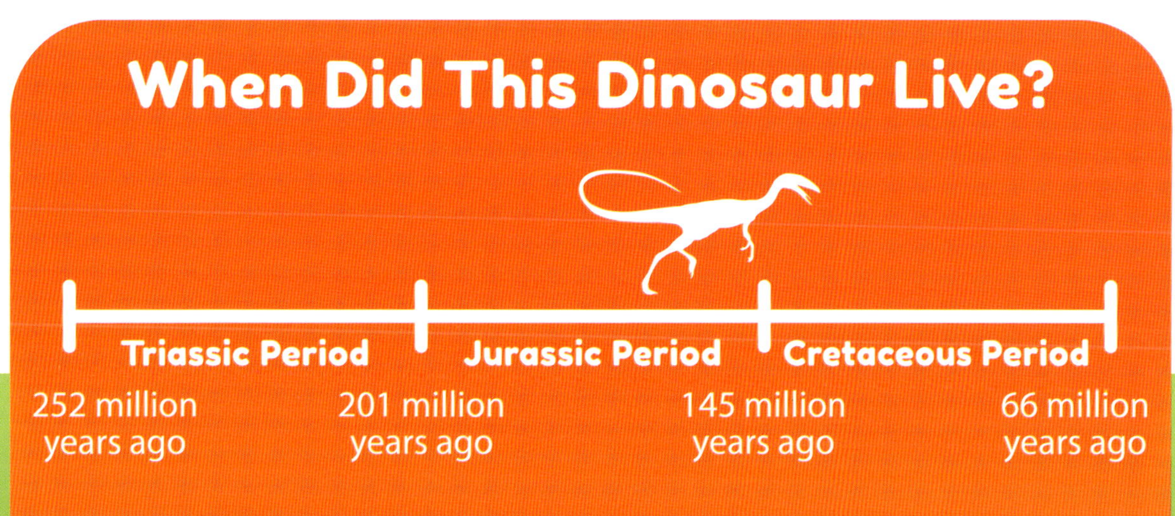

CONCAVENATOR

(kahn-KAY-veh-nay-tohr)

A New Discovery

In 2010, scientists announced that a new dinosaur had been discovered in Spain. It was *Concavenator*. This meat-eater lived during the Early Cretaceous Period.

Appearance

Concavenator had an unusual appearance. A triangular hump rose from low on its back, over its hips. Feathers may have sprouted from its short arms. At 20 feet (6.1 m) long and weighing around 2 tons (1.8 metric tons), it was a medium-sized theropod.

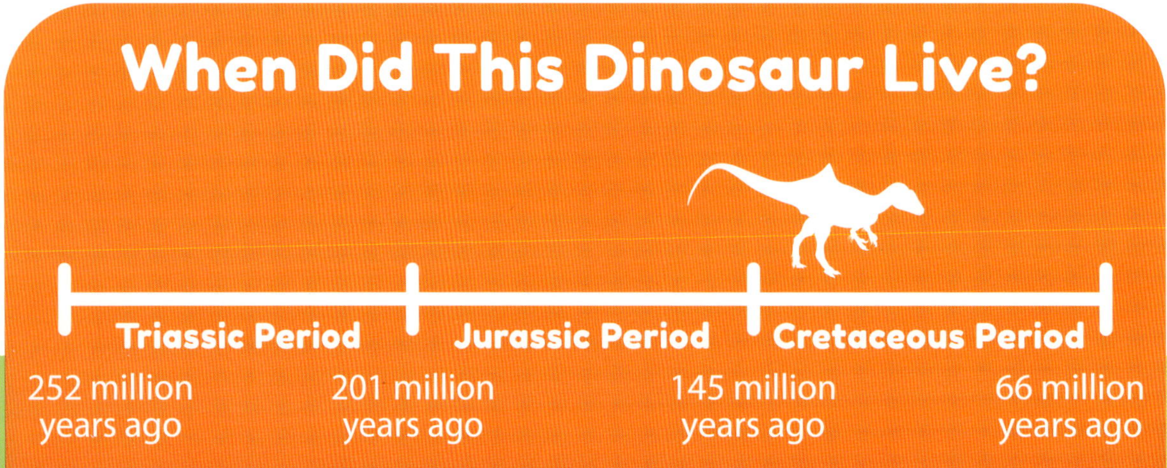

Concavenator fossil

Showing Off

Concavenator's odd features likely helped it show off to others of its own kind. Scientists call this *display*. The hump and feathers may have helped this dinosaur attract a mate. Or it may have used those features to threaten others of its kind. Then it could claim territory.

Length:
20 feet
(6.1 m)

Weight:
2 to 3 tons
(1.8 to 2.7 metric tons)

CRYOLOPHOSAURUS

(kreye-oh-LOH-fuh-SOHR-uhs)

Antarctic Dinosaur

Antarctica was not always freezing cold. During the Early Jurassic Period, it was covered in forests. The weather was cool. *Cryolophosaurus* was the top predator there. It was one of the earliest meat-eating dinosaurs.

Length:
26 feet
(8 m)

What Is in a Name?

Cryolophosaurus means "frozen crested reptile." *Frozen* honors its discovery in Antarctica.

Weight: 
1,100 pounds
(500 kg)

When Did This Dinosaur Live?

Triassic Period	Jurassic Period	Cretaceous Period
252 million years ago – 201 million years ago	201 million years ago – 145 million years ago	145 million years ago – 66 million years ago

Cryolophosaurus fossil

That is not an easy place to find fossils. *Crested* refers to the wide, curved crest above the dinosaur's eyes.

Appearance

The unusual head crest was this theropod's most interesting feature. It probably used the crest for display. The crest may have helped attract or threaten other dinosaurs. *Cryolophosaurus* hunted with its sharp, serrated teeth.

DEINOCHEIRUS

(DEYE-noh-KEYE-ruhs)

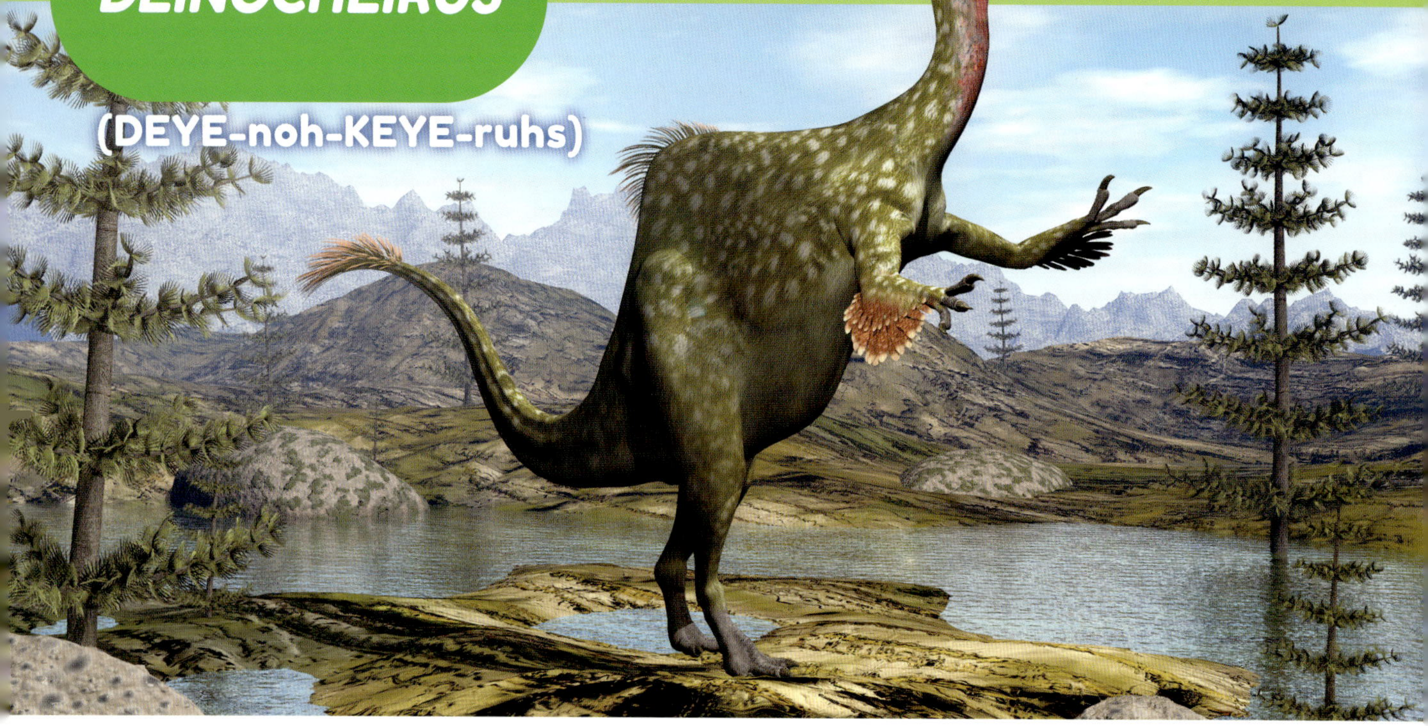

Terrible Hand

In the 1960s, scientists discovered a pair of huge dinosaur arms. They did not know what the rest of the dinosaur looked like. They called it

Length: 36 feet (11 m)

Weight: 6.6 tons (6 metric tons)

When Did This Dinosaur Live?

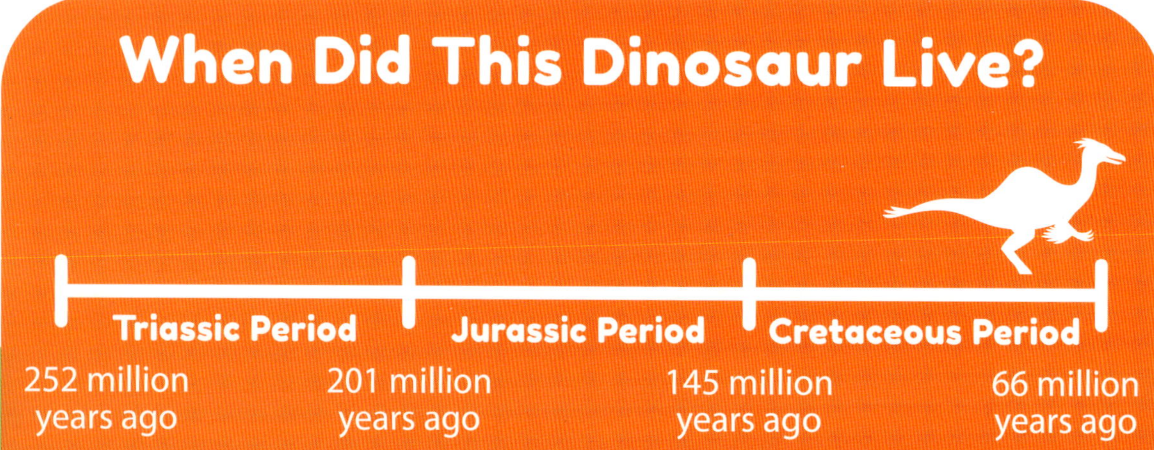

Deinocheirus. That means "terrible hand." In 2014, scientists finally found more fossils of *Deinocheirus*.

***Deinocheirus* arm bones**

Appearance

Deinocheirus grew to 36 feet (11 m) long. It weighed up to 6.6 tons (6 metric tons). That is bigger than most elephants. Its arms ended in three claws as long as bananas. A large hump rose from its back. It had a duck-like bill and square hooves on its toes.

At Home in the Mud

Deinocheirus probably scooped up plants from muddy rivers with its beak and claws. It also ate fish. It lived during the Late Cretaceous Period in what is now Mongolia.

DEINONYCHUS

(deye-NAHN-ih-kuhs)

Range

Deinonychus lived in what is now the United States. It was alive during the Cretaceous Period. It was a meat-eater. *Deinonychus* had a large brain. Scientists think this means it may have been smart.

Appearance

Deinonychus belongs to a group of bird-like dinosaurs commonly called raptors. One feature these dinosaurs shared was a large, curved talon extending from each foot. They used it as a weapon to slash and slice prey. The name *Deinonychus* means "terrible claw."

Length:
9.8 feet
(3 m)

Weight:
99 to 165 pounds
(45 to 75 kg)

A *Deinonychus* fossil is shown catching a young *Tenontosaurus.*

Scientists believe this dinosaur was covered in feathers.

Pack Attack

Deinonychus may have hunted in packs. These dinosaurs could work together to bring down large prey. Wolves and lions do this today.

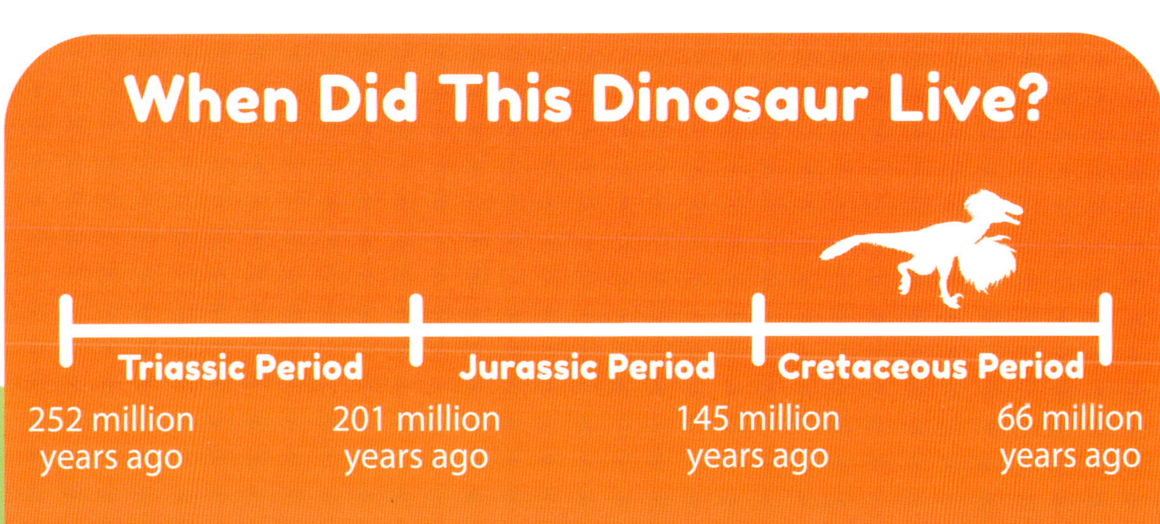

DILOPHOSAURUS

(deye-LOH-fuh-SOHR-uhs)

Jurassic Meat-Eater

Dilophosaurus lived during the Early Jurassic Period. It was one of the earliest large meat-eating dinosaurs. Jesse Williams was a member of the Navajo Nation. He found the first *Dilophosaurus* fossils on Navajo Nation land in the 1940s.

20 feet
(6 m)

Weight:
882 pounds
(400 kg)

Appearance

Twin crests popped out from the top of *Dilophosaurus*'s head. The crests were fragile. They were most likely used for display. *Dilophosaurus* was large compared to other dinosaurs that lived during its time period.

Dilophosaurus fossil

Movie Star

Dilophosaurus was in the *Jurassic Park* movies. It was shown as a small dinosaur. It flared a colorful frill and spat venom. But these features came from the imaginations of the movie creators. The real animal was large. There is no evidence it had a neck frill or spat venom.

DIPLODOCUS

(dih-PLAH-duh-kuhs)

Range

Diplodocus lived during the Late Jurassic Period in North America. It was one of the most common sauropods of its time. It likely traveled in small herds.

Appearance

Diplodocus was not the largest sauropod. But it was one of the longest. Its tail grew up to 43 feet (13 m) long. The whole dinosaur was longer than two school buses. It may have had a row of spines running down its back.

Length:
85 feet
(26 m)

Weight:
17 tons
(15 metric tons)

Diplodocus fossil

The Bone Wars

Othniel Marsh and Edward Cope were scientists who studied dinosaurs. In the late 1800s, they competed to collect fossils in the western United States. They spied on each other and stole each other's fossil finds. They discovered many dinosaurs, including *Diplodocus*, *Allosaurus*, and *Stegosaurus*.

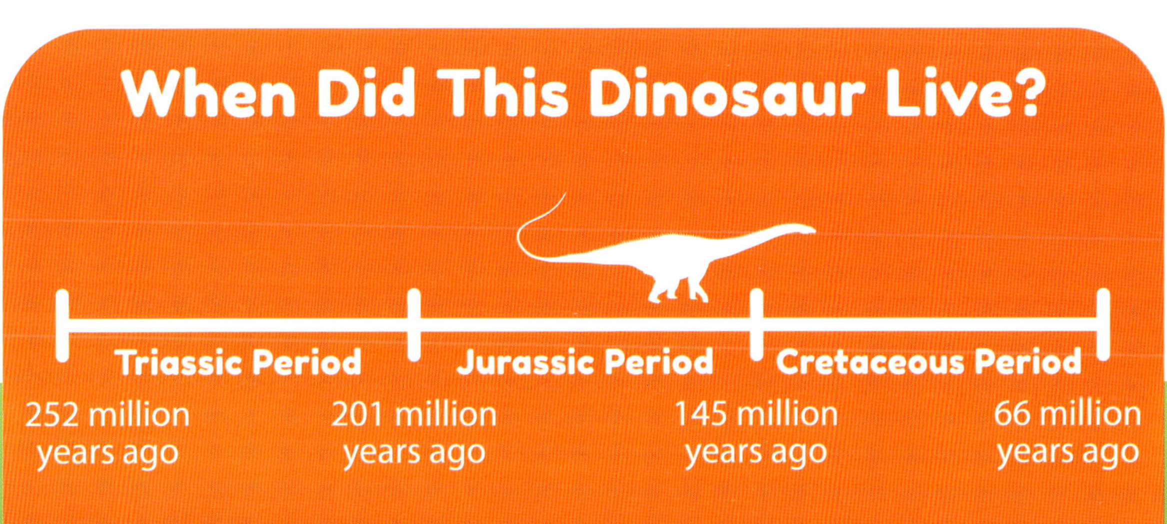

DREADNOUGHTUS

(drehd-NAHT-uhs)

Giant

In 2014, scientists announced the discovery of *Dreadnoughtus*. A *Dreadnoughtus* fossil found in 2005 was the most complete titanosaur ever found. This new dinosaur was also one of the biggest creatures to have ever lived on Earth. It lived during the Late Cretaceous Period in what is now South America.

Length:
85 feet
(26 m)

Weight:
65 tons
(59 metric tons)

Appearance

Dreadnoughtus's incredible size is difficult to imagine. This animal

When Did This Dinosaur Live?

Triassic Period	Jurassic Period	Cretaceous Period	
252 million years ago	201 million years ago	145 million years ago	66 million years ago

Scientist Kenneth Lacovara works with vertebrae, or backbone pieces, from *Dreadnoughtus*.

was heavier than a large airplane. It was twice as long as *Tyrannosaurus*.

Still Growing

A baby titanosaur hatched from an egg the size of a soccer ball. These dinosaurs grew to very large sizes. The bones of the only *Dreadnoughtus* found show that it was not yet an adult. If it had not died, it would have grown even larger.

EDMONTOSAURUS

(ehd-MAHN-tuh-SOHR-uhs)

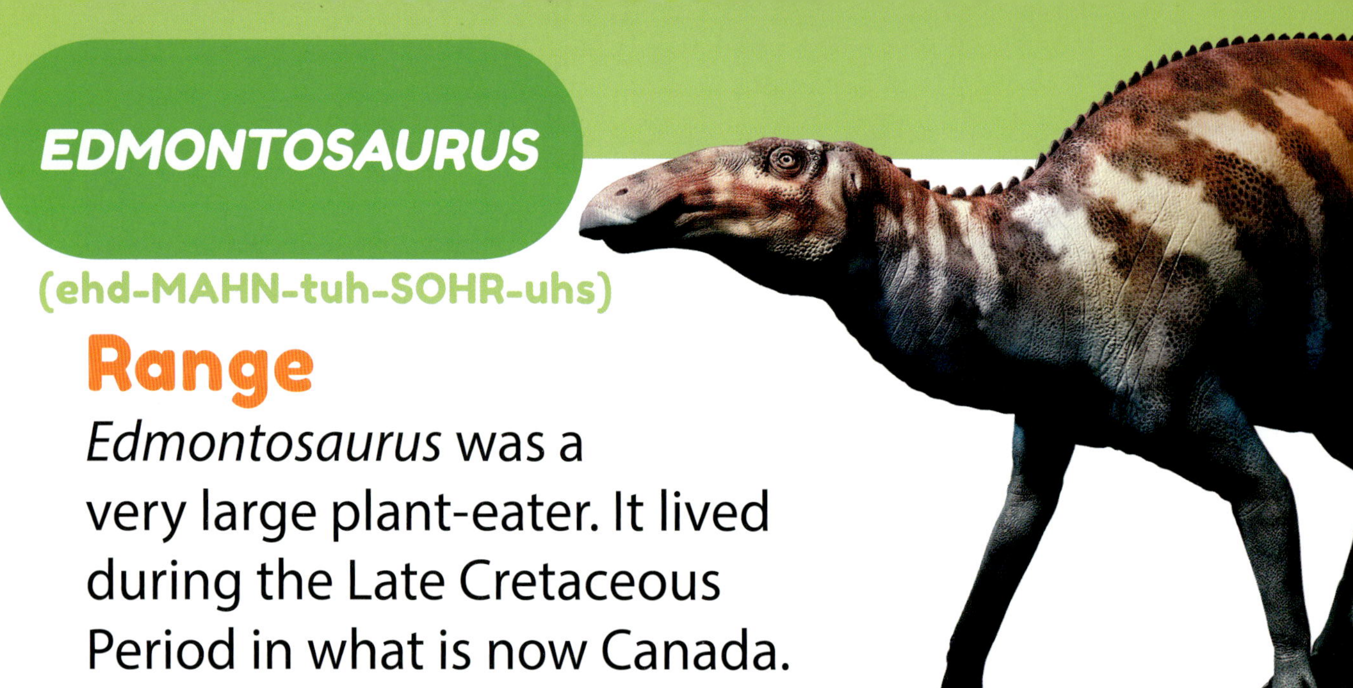

Range

Edmontosaurus was a very large plant-eater. It lived during the Late Cretaceous Period in what is now Canada. *Tyrannosaurus* hunted this dinosaur.

Appearance

Edmontosaurus was part of a group of dinosaurs called hadrosaurs. All hadrosaurs had duck-like bills and ate plants. *Edmontosaurus* was one of the largest and strongest in this group. It grew as long as a school bus. It had no teeth in the

Edmontosaurus fossil

bill at the front of its mouth. But sharp teeth for chewing filled the back of its mouth.

Pebbly Scales

In most dinosaur fossils, only the bones are left. One fossil of *Edmontosaurus* still has some preserved skin. The color has been lost. But the skin has a pebbly texture.

Length:
43 feet
(13 m)

Weight:

5.5 tons
(5 metric tons)

EUOPLOCEPHALUS

(YOO-oh-ploh-SEF-fuh-lus)

Range

Euoplocephalus was one of the most common dinosaurs of its time. It was around during the Late Cretaceous Period. It lived in what is now North America.

Length:
20 feet
(6.1 m)

Weight:
2 tons
(1.8 metric tons)

Appearance

Euoplocephalus was an ankylosaur. It had bony armor and spikes all over its body. This protected the dinosaur from predators.

When Did This Dinosaur Live?

Triassic Period | Jurassic Period | Cretaceous Period

252 million years ago | 201 million years ago | 145 million years ago | 66 million years ago

Euoplocephalus fossil

Even its eyelids had bony coverings. Its tail ended in a heavy club. *Euoplocephalus* could swing this club as a weapon. The club was strong enough to break the bones of other dinosaurs. *Euoplocephalus* was approximately the same length and weight as an elephant.

Digging for Food

Euoplocephalus had short, stubby legs that kept it close to the ground. This dinosaur ate plants. It likely also dug in the ground for roots.

GALLIMIMUS

(ga-luh-MEYE-muhs)

Range

Starting in the 1920s, fossil hunters began exploring the Gobi Desert in Mongolia. They made many exciting discoveries there. Zofia Kielan-Jaworowska was a Polish scientist. She found *Gallimimus* in 1964. This dinosaur lived during the Late Cretaceous Period.

Length: 20 feet (6.1 m)

Weight: 500 pounds (227 kg)

Appearance

The name *Gallimimus* means "chicken mimic." But this dinosaur was no chicken. It was twice the size of an ostrich. Like an ostrich, it ran very fast on two legs. It also had a toothless beak. *Gallimimus* likely used its beak to eat tiny animals and plants found in water.

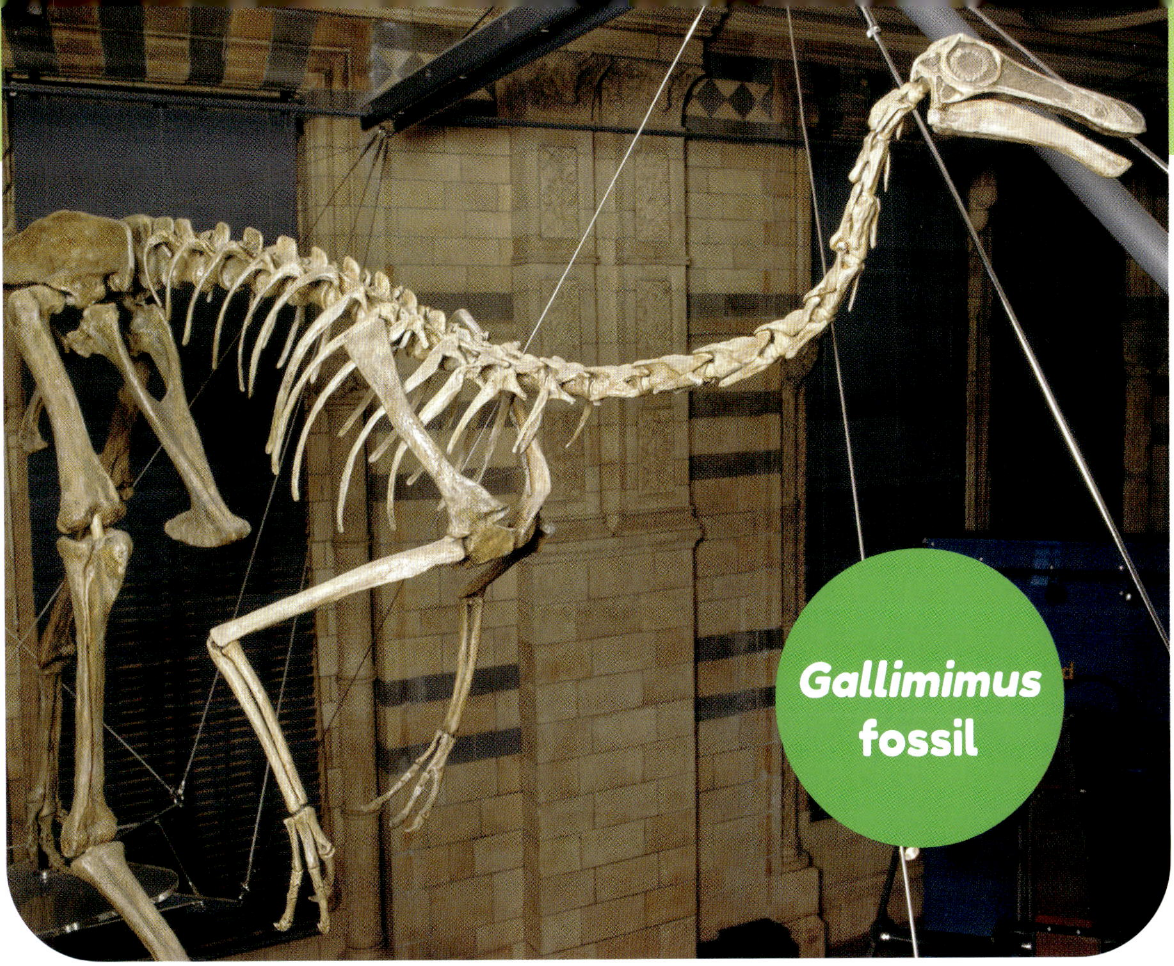

Gallimimus fossil

The Eyes Have It

Gallimimus's eyes were on either side of its head. They could see in different directions at the same time. But they could not judge distance very well.

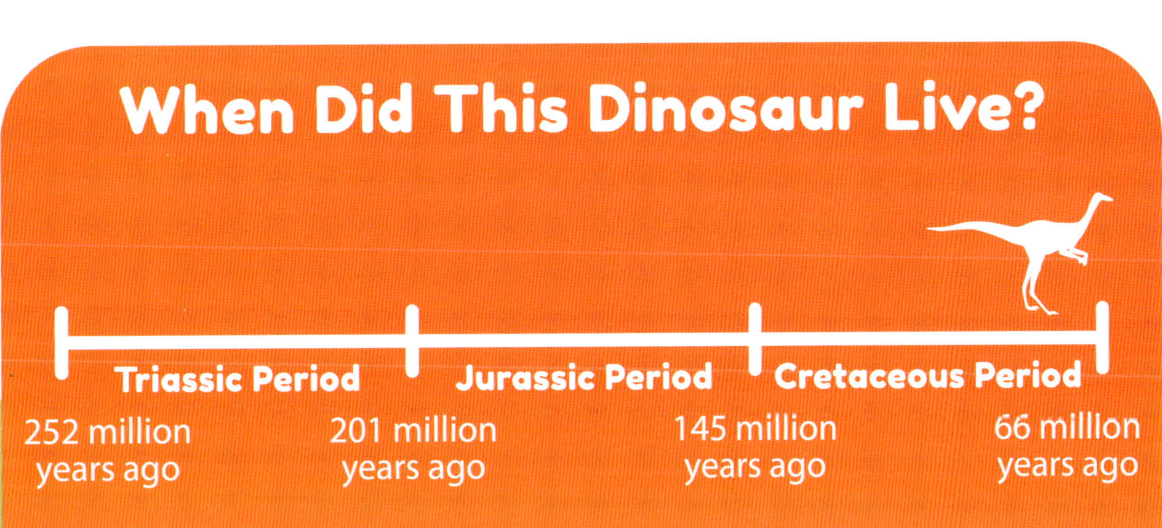

GIGANOTOSAURUS

(gig-uh-NOH-toh-SOHR-uhs)

Range

In 1993, a fossil hunter named Rubén Carolini found a large dinosaur skull in Argentina. It turned out to belong to *Giganotosaurus*. This huge, meat-eating theropod lived during the Cretaceous Period.

Appearance

Giganotosaurus was even bigger and heavier than *Tyrannosaurus*. Its head alone was 6 feet (1.8 m) long. Its jagged teeth were 8 inches (20 cm) long. The only meat-eater known to be larger is *Spinosaurus*.

When Did This Dinosaur Live?

Triassic Period | Jurassic Period | Cretaceous Period

252 million years ago

201 million years ago

145 million years ago

66 million years ago

Giganotosaurus skeleton

Mighty Hunter

Giganotosaurus was fast. It likely reached speeds of 31 miles per hour (50 kmh). It lived in family groups. These groups may have hunted together to take down titanosaurs. Scientists think *Giganotosaurus* might have hunted *Argentinosaurus*.

Length:
46 feet
(14 m)

Weight:
8.8 tons
(8 metric tons)

GIGANTORAPTOR

(jeye-GAN-toh-rap-ter)

Range

Paleontologist Xing Xu and a team of scientists from China discovered *Gigantoraptor* in Mongolia. They announced the giant, bird-like dinosaur in 2007. It lived during the end of the Cretaceous Period.

Appearance

This massive dinosaur was about as tall as a car is long. It weighed up to 1.4 tons (1.3 metric tons). It is the largest dinosaur with a beak ever discovered. It also laid the

When Did This Dinosaur Live?

Triassic Period | Jurassic Period | Cretaceous Period

252 million years ago
201 million years ago
145 million years ago
66 million years ago

Fossilized *Gigantoraptor* bones in China

largest dinosaur eggs yet found. It may have had feathers.

Mystery Diet

Only one fossil of *Gigantoraptor* has been found. Scientists do not know what this giant ate. It probably ate plants and fruit. It may have eaten some small animals as well.

Length:
26 feet
(7.9 m)

Weight:
1.4 tons
(1.3 metric tons)

(jih-RAF-uh-teye-tehn)

Museum Giant

Giraffatitan was a huge sauropod. It ate from treetops during the Late Jurassic Period. Scientists dug up a *Giraffatitan* fossil in Tanzania in the early 1900s. Today, a museum in Germany shows off the fossil to visitors. It is the tallest dinosaur fossil shown to the public.

***Giraffatitan* skeleton at the Natural History Museum in Berlin, Germany**

Appearance

The name *Giraffatitan* means "giant giraffe." This dinosaur had a long neck and grew to a gigantic size. It was as tall as a four-story building. Its body shape was similar to a giraffe's.

Name Change

For a long time, people thought *Giraffatitan* was a *Brachiosaurus*. In the late 1900s, some scientists figured out that it was a different dinosaur. *Brachiosaurus* has a smoothly sloping snout. *Giraffatitan* has a curved snout and a high forehead.

Length:
80 feet
(24 m)

Weight:
40 tons
(36 metric tons)

When Did This Dinosaur Live?

Triassic Period	Jurassic Period	Cretaceous Period

252 million years ago — 201 million years ago — 145 million years ago — 66 million years ago

HADROSAURUS

(ha-droh-SOHR-uhs)

Early Discovery

Hadrosaurus was one of the first dinosaurs that scientists discovered. In 1868, it became the first dinosaur ever shown at a museum. *Hadrosaurus* was found in New Jersey. It is the official state fossil there. This large plant-eater lived during the Late Cretaceous Period.

Appearance

Hadrosaurus was similar in size to a large elephant. It gave its name to an entire group of dinosaurs called hadrosaurs. They were all plant-eaters with duck-like bills. A *Hadrosaurus* skull has never been found. Scientists assume it had a bill like its cousins.

Length:
23 to 33 feet
(7 to 10 m)

Weight:
2.2 to 3.3 tons
(2 to 3 metric tons)

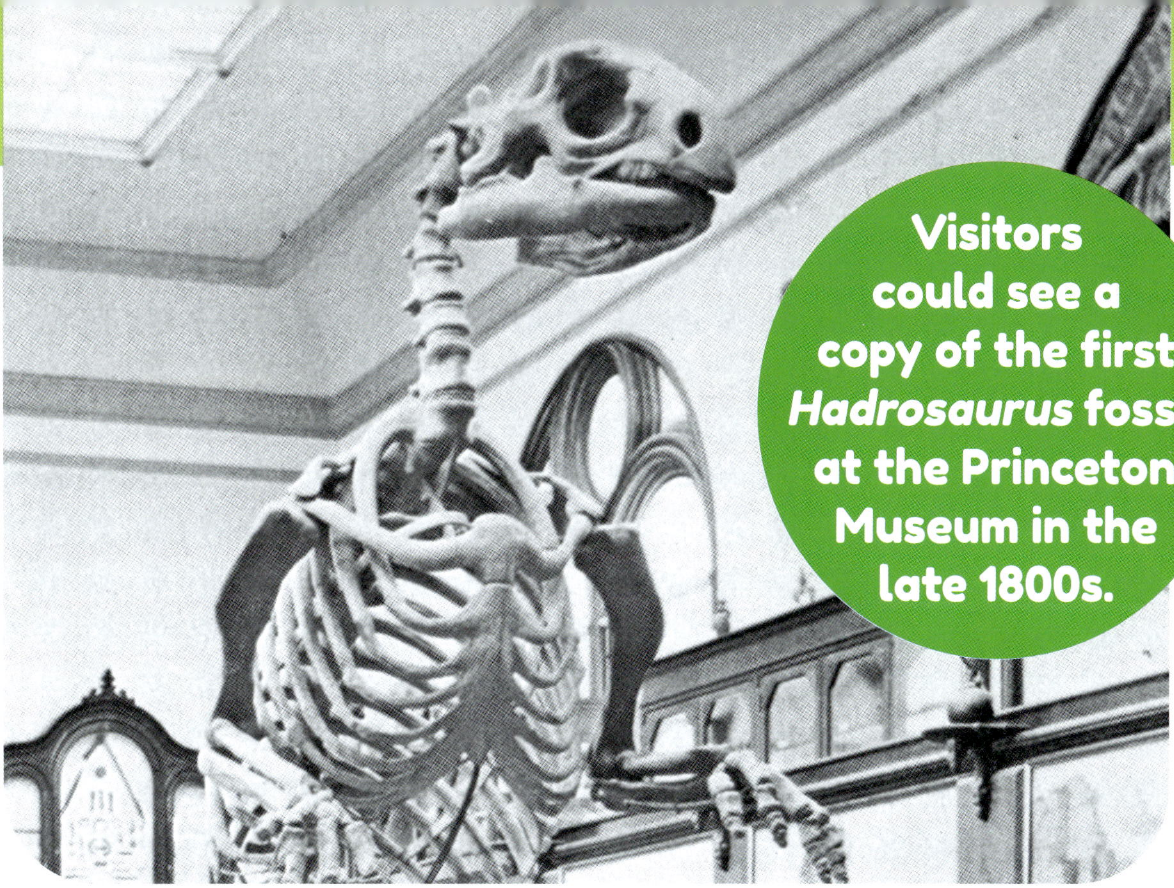

Visitors could see a copy of the first *Hadrosaurus* fossil at the Princeton Museum in the late 1800s.

Huge Grazer

Hadrosaurus could run on its two powerful hind legs. But most of the time, it stood on all four legs to graze on plants. It likely lived in small groups called herds.

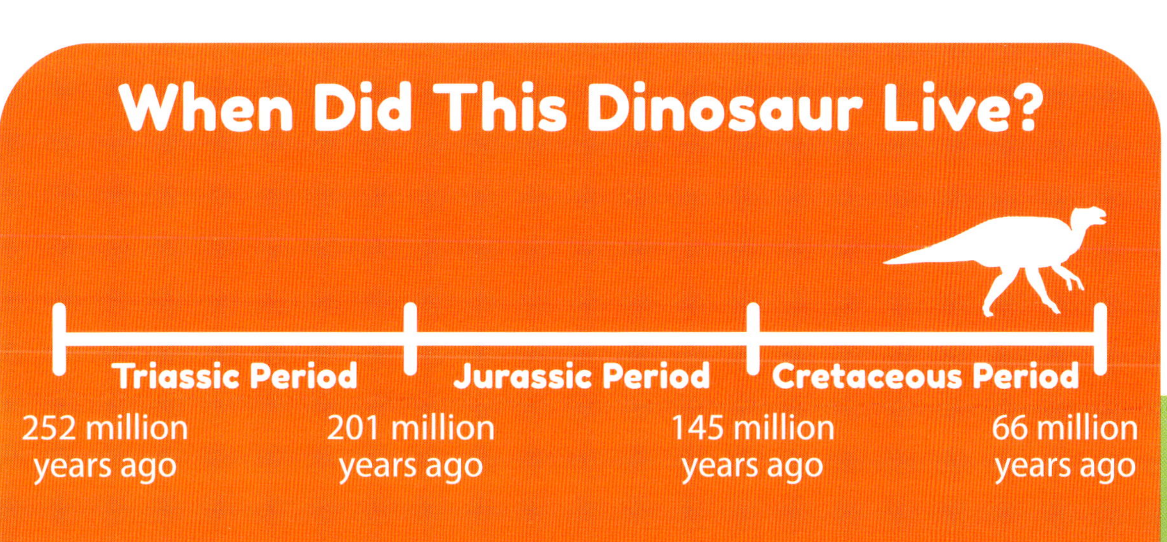

HERRERASAURUS

(heh-REH-ruh-SOHR-uhs)

Early Dinosaur

Herrerasaurus was one of the earliest dinosaurs. This theropod lived more than 200 million years ago. This was during the Late Triassic Period. *Herrerasaurus* fossils were an important find for scientists. These fossils revealed how theropods first evolved.

Length:
9.8 feet
(3 m)

Weight:
400 pounds
(180 kg)

Appearance

Herrerasaurus was a bit larger than a wolf. It was a hunter. This dinosaur ran on its two hind legs. Its long tail helped it balance and turn. That type of tail was one of the first features to evolve in theropods. *Herrerasaurus*'s ear bones show that it had excellent hearing.

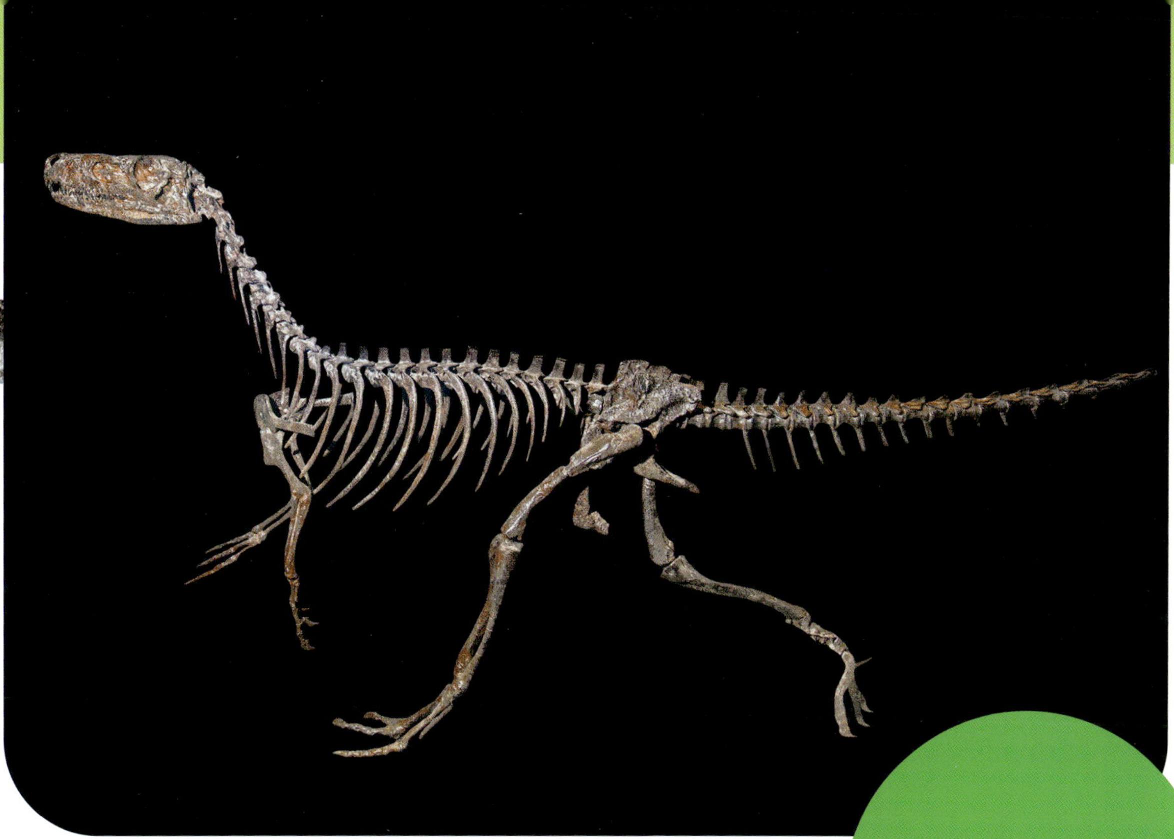

Herrerasaurus fossil

Namesake

A farmer found the first *Herrerasaurus* fossil in Argentina in 1958. His name was Victorino Herrera. Scientists named the dinosaur after him.

When Did This Dinosaur Live?

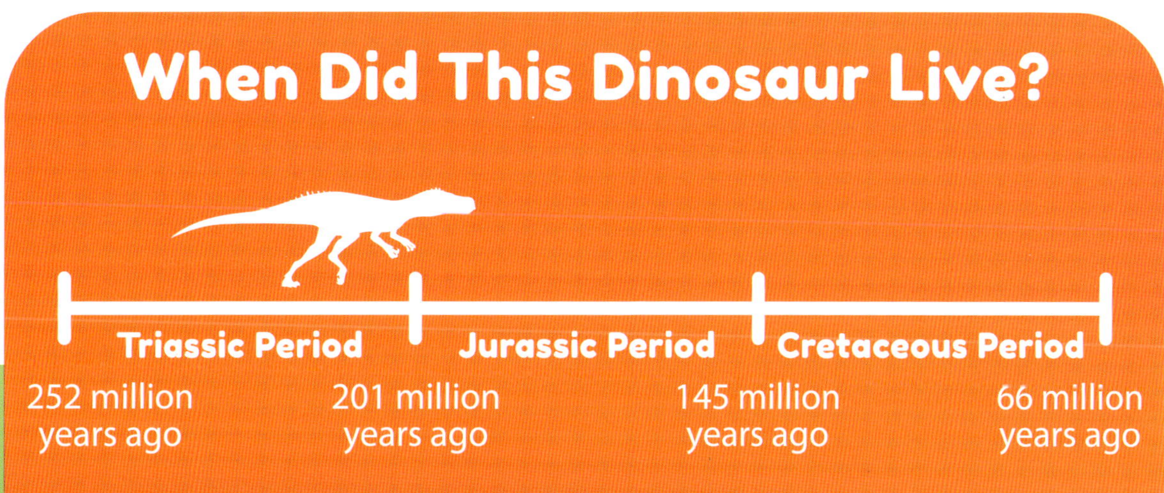

HETERODONTOSAURUS

(heh-ter-oh-DAHN-tuh-SOHR-uhs)

Range

Scientists have found several very detailed fossils of *Heterodontosaurus* in South Africa. This dinosaur was small. It lived during the Early Jurassic Period.

Appearance

Heterodontosaurus grew no bigger than a medium-sized dog. It was about 4 feet (1.3 m) long. It weighed around 44 pounds (20 kg). It ran on two long back legs. Its hands had five fingers. *Heterodontosaurus* used its fingers to grab things.

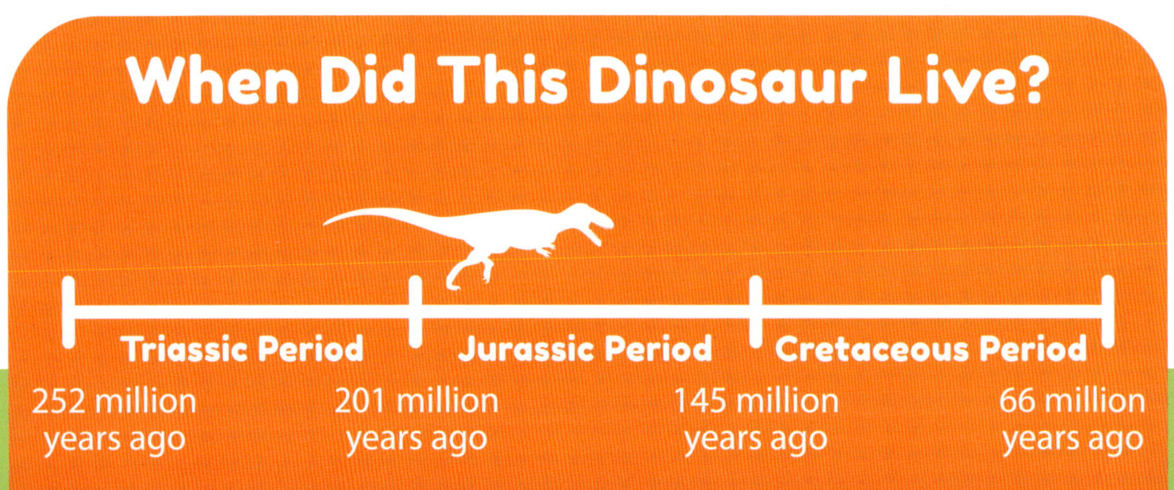

***Heterodontosaurus* fossil**

Two Tusks

Two sharp tusks stuck up from this dinosaur's bottom jaw. That may have made it look a bit like a wild boar. It also had flat teeth for chewing and sharp teeth for biting. *Heterodontosaurus* means "different-teeth reptile." This dinosaur may have eaten both meat and plants.

Length:
4 feet
(1.3 m)

Weight:
44 pounds
(20 kg)

IGUANODON

(ih-GWAH-nuh-dahn)

Range

Iguanodon was one of the first dinosaurs ever discovered. It was alive during the Early Cretaceous Period. It lived in what is now Europe.

Length:
33 feet
(10 m)

Weight:
5 tons
(4.5 metric tons)

Mysterious Teeth

In 1822, Mary Ann Mantell was traveling with her husband in England. She noticed large teeth fossils on the side of the road. The Mantells thought they looked like massive iguana teeth.

When Did This Dinosaur Live?

Triassic Period		Jurassic Period		Cretaceous Period	
252 million years ago		201 million years ago		145 million years ago	66 million years ago

Iguanodon fossil

They named the animal *Iguanodon*. The teeth helped prove that dinosaurs existed.

Appearance

Iguanodon was a very large plant-eater. It was almost as tall and heavy as an elephant. But its neck and tail made it longer than an elephant. It had a beak-like mouth and walked on four feet. Its front feet each had a sharp spike. Early scientists mistakenly thought this spike belonged on *Iguanodon*'s nose.

KENTROSAURUS

(KEHN-truh-SOHR-uhs)

Range

Scientists found hundreds of *Kentrosaurus* fossils in the early 1900s. The fossils were in Tanzania. The scientists thought that around 70 of these plant-eaters died at once. The dinosaurs were likely traveling in a herd. *Kentrosaurus* lived during the Late Jurassic Period.

Length:
16 feet
(5 m)

Weight:
2.2 tons
(2 metric tons)

Appearance

Kentrosaurus looked like its cousin *Stegosaurus*. Both dinosaurs had long back legs and short front legs. They both had small heads and tiny brains. *Kentrosaurus* was smaller. It had narrower back plates and more spikes. Two long spikes

Kentrosaurus fossil

jutted out from its sides. It was similar in size to a large rhinoceros.

A Mighty Weapon

A scientist made a computer model of *Kentrosaurus*. The model showed that it could swing its tail hard enough to break bones. The spikes on the tail could slash or pierce skin.

KOSMOCERATOPS

(KAHZ-moh-SEH-ruh-tahps)

Range

Kosmoceratops lived in what is now North America. It was alive during the Late Cretaceous Period. It belongs to a group of dinosaurs called ceratopsians. They were all plant-eaters that walked on four legs. Most had horns and frills.

Length:
15 feet
(4.6 m)

Weight: 
1 to 2 tons
(0.9 to
1.8 metric tons)

Appearance

Fifteen horns sprouted from the frill of a *Kosmoceratops*. That

When Did This Dinosaur Live?

Kosmoceratops skull

is the most horns ever found on a dinosaur's head. Many of those horns curved forward. They formed an unusual wave-like shape at the top of the frill. *Kosmoceratops* was approximately the same size as a large rhinoceros.

Beauty Contest

Most likely, fancier frills attracted mates. *Kosmoceratops* may have used its horns to fight for mates. It may also have fought for a higher rank in a herd. Horned deer do this today.

LAMBEOSAURUS

(LAM-bee-oh-SOHR-uhs)

Range

Lambeosaurus was a hadrosaur. It lived during the Late Cretaceous Period. It roamed over a wide area along the western coast of what is now North America.

Appearance

Like other hadrosaurs, *Lambeosaurus* ate plants. It had a duck-like bill. *Lambeosaurus* had no teeth in its beak. But there were many teeth in the back of its mouth. A hollow crest stuck out of the top of *Lambeosaurus*'s head. The crest was shaped like the bill of a baseball cap.

Length:
30 to 54 feet
(9 to 16.5 m)

Weight: 
20 tons
(18 metric tons)

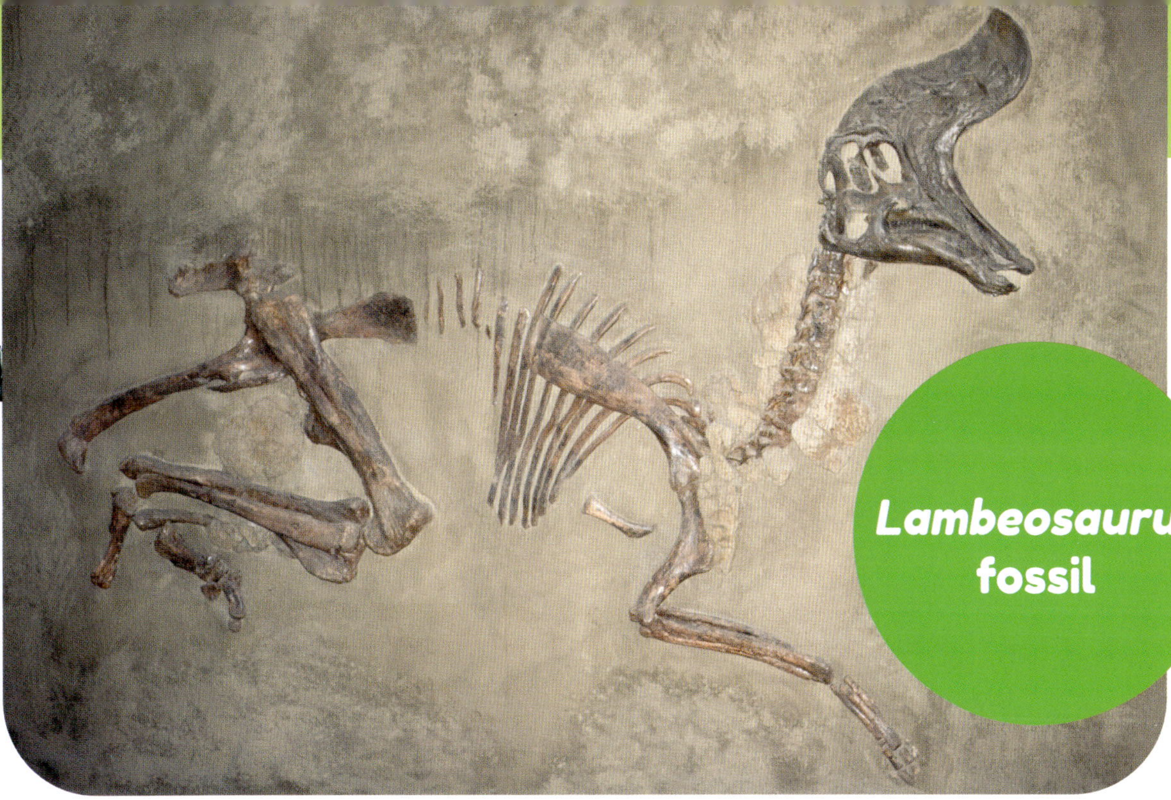

Lambeosaurus fossil

The Crest Mystery

Lambeosaurus may have used its crest for display. The hollow part of the crest connected to the dinosaur's nose. This means it may have used the crest to make loud sounds. Or it may have had an excellent sense of smell.

When Did This Dinosaur Live?

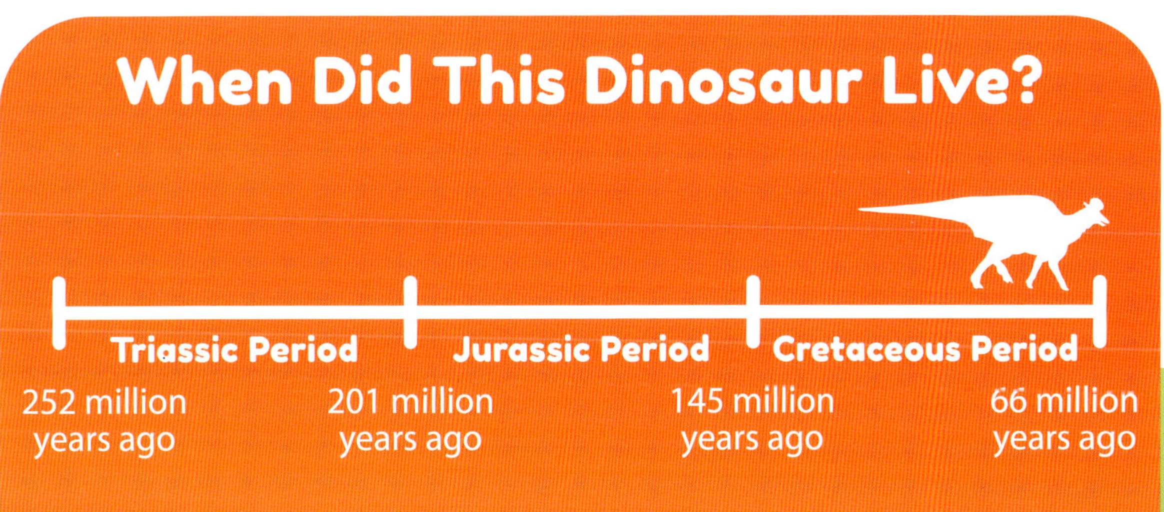

MAIASAURA

(MEYE-uh-SOHR-uh)

Range

Maiasaura was a hadrosaur. It lived at the very end of the Cretaceous Period. Herds that may have included thousands of *Maiasaura* lived together in what is now North America.

Length: 30 feet (9 m)

Weight:  4.4 tons (4 metric tons)

Appearance

Maiasaura was about the same size as an elephant. It had a long head with a small ridge over each eye. It ate plants with a

When Did This Dinosaur Live?

Triassic Period | Jurassic Period | Cretaceous Period

252 million years ago | 201 million years ago | 145 million years ago | 66 million years ago

Maiasaura fossil

duck-like bill. It likely walked on four legs while grazing. But it could run on two legs.

A Caring Mother

In the 1970s, scientists found the first *Maiasaura* fossils. They recovered nests, eggs, eggshells, babies, and adults. The fossils told the scientists about the dinosaur. These dinosaurs must have nested in large groups. They also cared for their young. The scientists chose the name *Maiasaura*. It means "good mother reptile."

MAJUNGASAURUS

(muh-JOON-guh-SOHR-uhs)

Range

Majungasaurus was a meat-eater. It was around at the end of the Cretaceous Period. It lived on what is now the island of Madagascar. It was the largest hunter there.

Appearance

Majungasaurus was similar in size to a small elephant. It grew to 20 feet (6.1 m) long. Like other theropods, it ran quickly on two legs. It had very short arms. A single, small horn grew on top of its head. *Majungasaurus* had a short snout.

A museum in California shows *Majungasaurus, left,* fighting *Rapetosaurus.*

Unusual Eating Habits

This dinosaur most likely hunted plant-eaters, including long-necked sauropods. But scientists have found out that it also ate its own kind. This is called cannibalism. Scientists do not know if the dinosaur did this all the time or only in difficult situations.

Length:
20 feet
(6.1 m)

Weight:
1 ton
(0.9 metric tons)

MAMENCHISAURUS

(muh-MEHN-chee-SOHR-uhs)

Range

The Chinese scientist Yang Zhongjian announced the discovery of *Mamenchisaurus* in 1954. This giant sauropod lived in what is now China. It lived during the Late Jurassic Period.

Length:
72 to 82 feet
(22 to 25 m)

Weight:
13 to 16.5 tons
(12 to 15 metric tons)

Appearance

Mamenchisaurus had one of the longest necks of any dinosaur. Its neck stretched up to 40 feet (12 m) long. That was almost half the dinosaur's total body length. This dinosaur

When Did This Dinosaur Live?

Triassic Period | Jurassic Period | Cretaceous Period

252 million years ago
201 million years ago
145 million years ago
66 million years ago

Mamenchisaurus* fossil, *top

had 19 neck bones. Long-necked animals living today have fewer neck bones. For example, giraffes have only seven bones in their necks.

Long Neck

Some scientists think *Mamenchisaurus* could not lift its super-long neck up high. It is possible that it swung its neck from side to side to find plants to eat. It may have grazed like a huge lawn trimmer.

MASSOSPONDYLUS

(mas-oh-SPAHN-dih-luhs)

Egg Fossils

In 1976, scientists found dinosaur egg fossils in South Africa. They belonged to *Massospondylus.* It laid the eggs around 190 million years ago. That was during the Early Jurassic Period. They are among the oldest dinosaur eggs ever found.

16 feet
(5 m)

Weight:
772 pounds
(350 kg)

Appearance

Massospondylus had a long neck, a small head, and a long tail. Babies walked on four legs. Adults walked on two legs. *Massospondylus* grew to 16 feet (5 m) long. That was small compared to its descendants. They were the gigantic sauropods.

A scientist puts together a *Massospondylus* skeleton.

Stomach Stones

Scientists found stones in a *Massospondylus* stomach fossil. Some birds today swallow stones to help break down the plants they eat. *Massospondylus* might have done the same thing. This dinosaur also had sharp teeth. It likely ate plants and some meat.

MICRORAPTOR

(MEYE-kroh-rap-ter)

Range

Microraptor was a bird-like dinosaur. It hunted in treetops in what is now China. It ate birds and other small animals. It lived during the Early Cretaceous Period.

Appearance

Microraptor is one of the smallest dinosaurs ever found. It was around the size of a crow. One type of *Microraptor* even had shiny, black feathers. Unlike a bird, it had four wings and a long, feathered tail. It also had teeth in its beak.

Microraptor fossil

High Flier

Many dinosaurs grew feathers for warmth. *Microraptor* used its feathers to glide long distances. It may have been able to fly very short distances. A flying animal flaps its wings to lift itself off the ground. A glider leaps into the air and soars like a kite. *Microraptor* represents an important link between gliding and flying.

Length:
2.6 feet
(0.8 m)

Weight:
2.2 pounds
(1 kg)

MINMI

(MIHN-mee)

Range

Minmi was an ankylosaur. It lived in what is now Australia. It was one of the most common dinosaurs in this area during the Early Cretaceous Period.

Length: 10 feet (3 m)

Weight: 882 pounds (400 kg)

Appearance

Minmi was a small, armored dinosaur that walked on four legs. It was about the same size as an alligator. Unlike most of its ankylosaur cousins, *Minmi* had

When Did This Dinosaur Live?

Triassic Period	Jurassic Period	Cretaceous Period	
252 million years ago	201 million years ago	145 million years ago	66 million years ago

Visitors to the Melbourne Museum in Australia see how they measure up to a life-sized *Minmi* model.

long legs. It likely had strong back muscles. This means it was probably a fast runner. Knobby armor covered its body and belly. It had short spikes along its tail. Its head and brain were quite small for its size.

Fern Salad

Minmi had a toothless beak. It used teeth in the back of its mouth to chew up plants. It feasted on seeds, ferns, and other low-growing plants.

MUTTABURRASAURUS

(MUH-tuh-BER-uh-SOHR-uhs)

Australian Dinosaur

Muttaburrasaurus was a large plant-eater. It lived during the Cretaceous Period. This was the first Australian dinosaur fossil that people could see in a museum.

Appearance

Muttaburrasaurus had a big nose. This was because of a hollow, rounded bone over its snout. This feature may have helped the dinosaur make noise. Or perhaps the dinosaur had an excellent sense of smell. This dinosaur also had a duck-like bill. *Muttaburrasaurus* had spikes on its thumbs. It could walk on two or four legs. It was similar in size to an elephant.

Length: 23 feet (7 m)

Weight: 3.3 tons (3 metric tons)

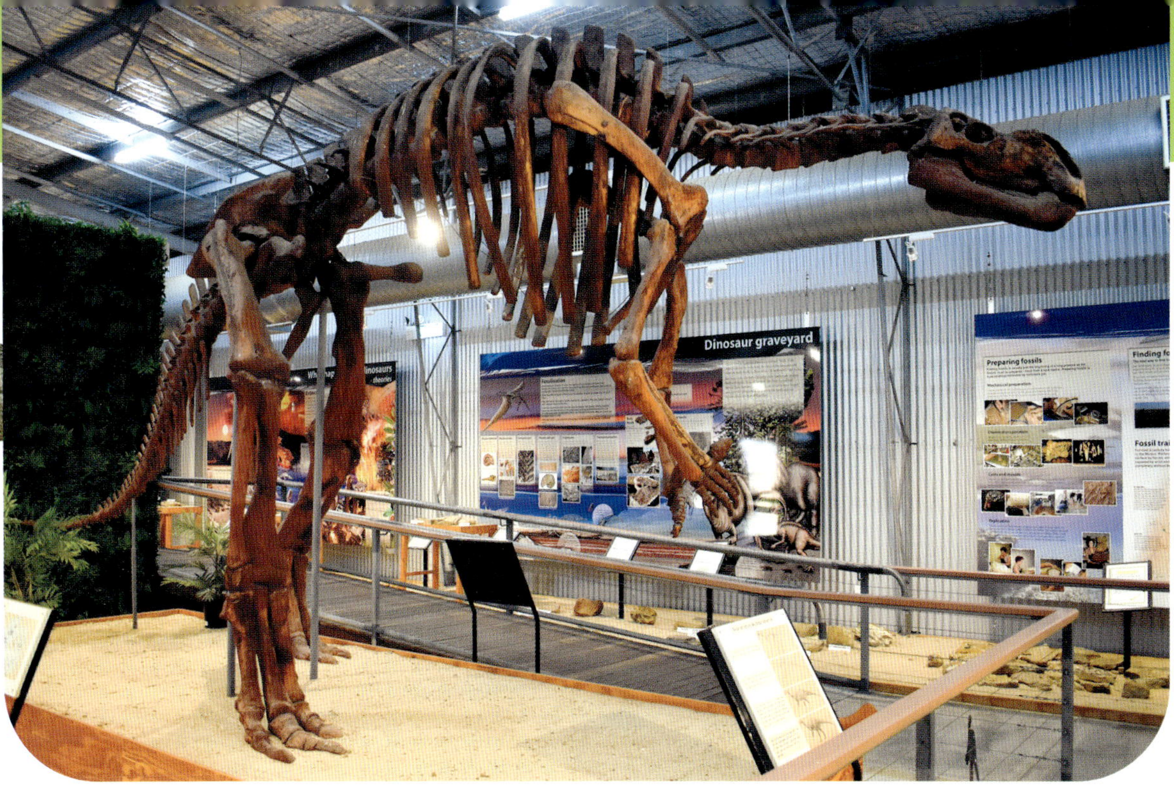

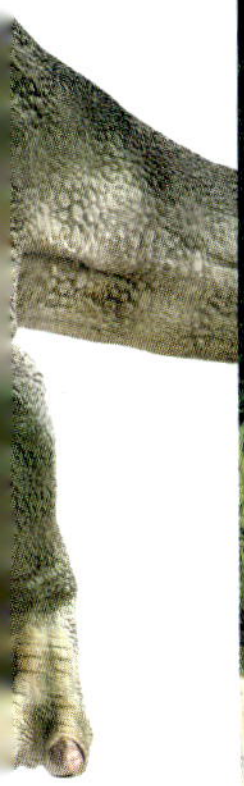

Muttaburrasaurus fossil

Ancient Ocean

During the Cretaceous Period, most of what is now Australia was covered by ocean. *Muttaburrasaurus* lived in forests near the ocean. It likely ate ferns and other low-growing plants.

When Did This Dinosaur Live?

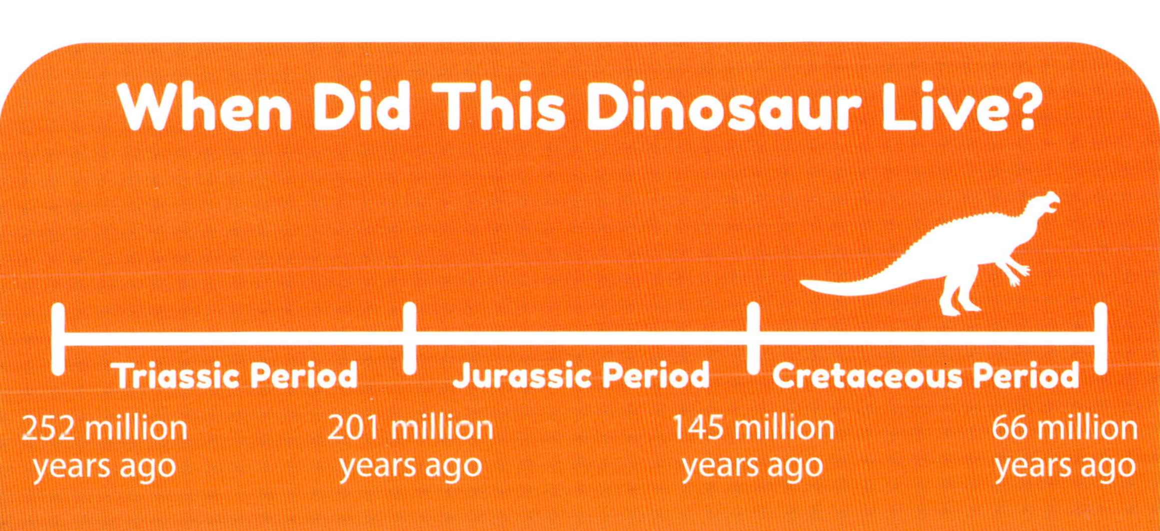

NIGERSAURUS

(NEE-zhehr-SOHR-uhs)

Range

Rivers once flowed in the area that is now the Sahara Desert. This was more than 100 million years ago, during the Early Cretaceous Period. Many dinosaurs lived in this area. One was *Nigersaurus*. It was named for Niger, the country where its fossils were first found.

Appearance

Nigersaurus was a sauropod. It was bigger than an elephant. But it was still smaller than most of its sauropod cousins. *Nigersaurus* had a large, flat mouth that was wider than its head. Paul Sereno is the scientist who discovered the dinosaur. He thought its skull looked like Darth Vader's helmet.

Length:
30 feet
(9.1 m)

Weight:
5 tons
(4.5 metric tons)

Paul Sereno poses with a *Nigersaurus* skull.

Ancient Lawn Mower

More than 500 straight, skinny teeth filled *Nigersaurus*'s jaws. It likely swung its head across the ground. Then it could chomp plants like a lawn mower.

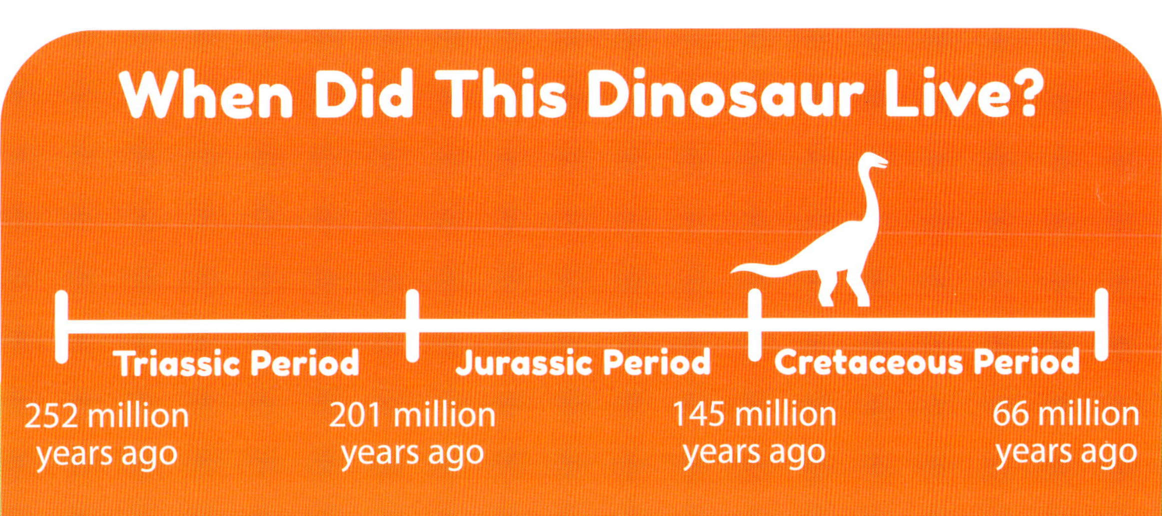

OVIRAPTOR

(OH-vih-rap-ter)

Range

Oviraptor was a bird-like dinosaur from the Late Cretaceous Period. It lived in what is now Asia. In 2021, scientists found a baby *Oviraptor* preserved inside an egg fossil.

Length: 6.6 feet (2 m)

Weight: 66 pounds (30 kg)

Appearance

Oviraptor's strong, toothless beak resembled a parrot's. The dinosaur was about the same size as a large dog. A crest rose from the top of its head. *Oviraptor* ran on two strong back legs. This dinosaur most likely used its beak to crush shellfish. It may have also eaten plants and small animals.

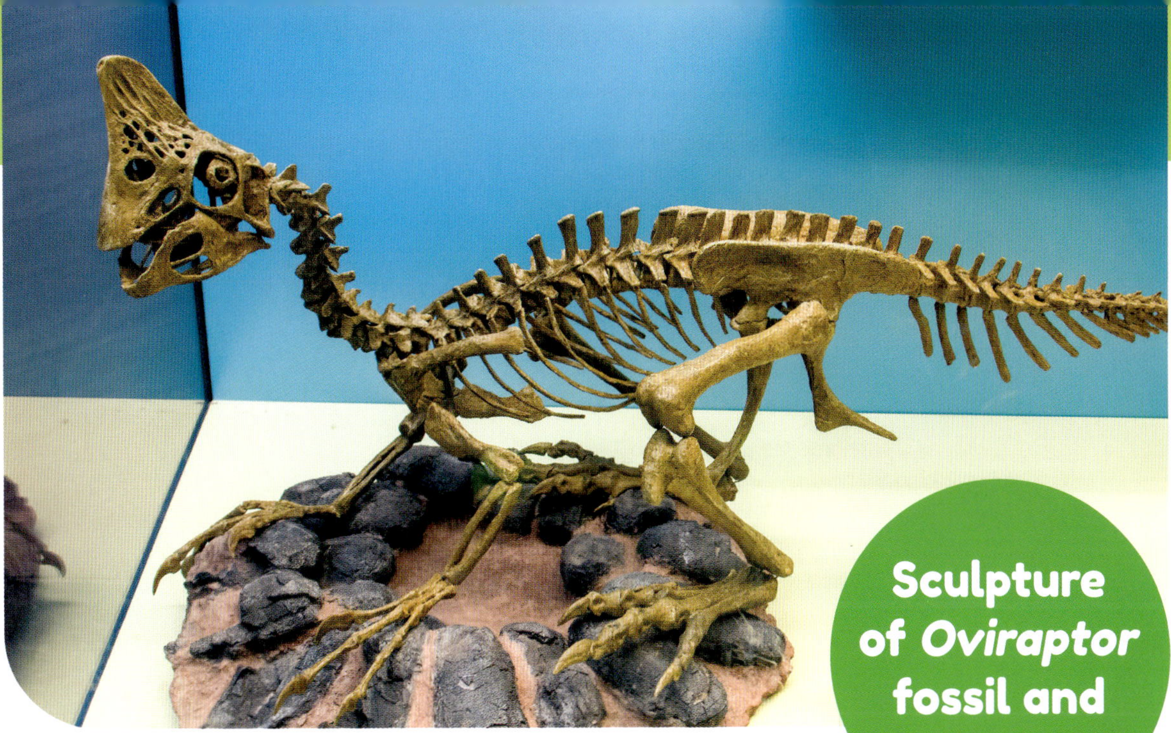

Sculpture of *Oviraptor* fossil and its eggs

Not Guilty!

The name *Oviraptor* means "egg thief." Scientists found its fossils next to a group of eggs. At first, they thought the *Oviraptor* had been stealing those eggs to eat. Scientists later learned they were the *Oviraptor*'s own eggs. The dinosaur was not a thief after all.

When Did This Dinosaur Live?

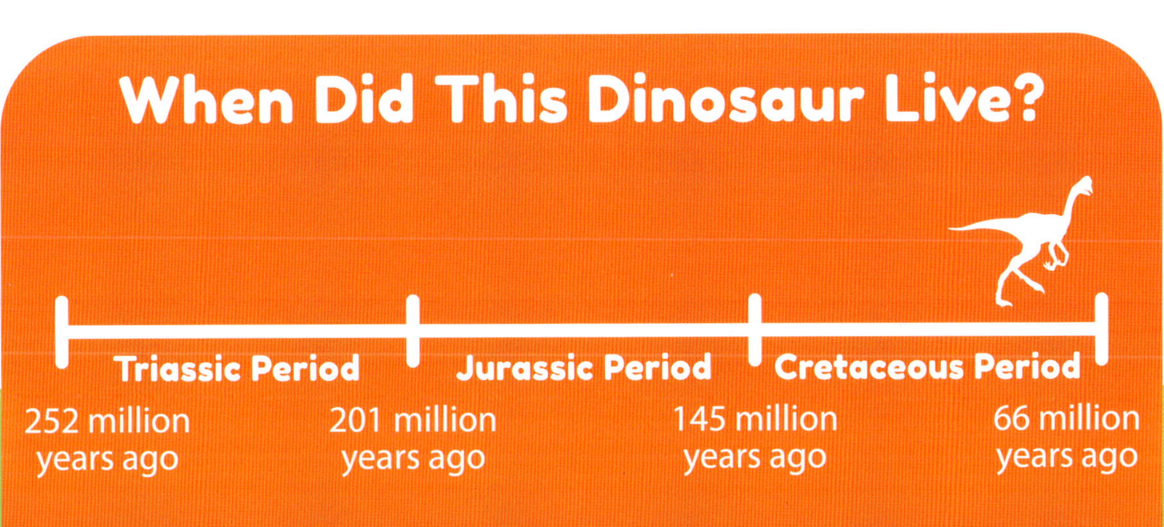

PACHYCEPHALOSAURUS

(pack-ee-SEH-fuh-loh-SOHR-uhs)

Range

Pachycephalosaurus lived in what is now North America. It likely ate plants, fruits, seeds, and bugs. It was probably around for the asteroid strike that ended the Cretaceous Period.

Length:
26 feet
(8 m)

Appearance

Pachycephalosaurus means "thick head reptile." This dinosaur is famous for the bony dome on top of its head. Spikes stuck out from the back of the dome and the top of the dinosaur's nose.

Weight:
3.3 tons
(3 metric tons)

When Did This Dinosaur Live?

Triassic Period
Jurassic Period
Cretaceous Period

252 million years ago
201 million years ago
145 million years ago
66 million years ago

***Pachycephalosaurus* fossil**

Scientists used to think these dinosaurs butted heads. Now they think the dome was too fragile for this. It was likely for display.

Growing Up

In 2006, scientists announced a new dinosaur named *Dracorex hogwartsia*. It was named after Hogwarts, the wizard school in the *Harry Potter* series. Later research showed that *Dracorex* was just a young *Pachycephalosaurus*.

PACHYRHINOSAURUS

(pack-ee-REYE-noh-SOHR-uhs)

Range

Near the end of the Cretaceous Period, *Pachyrhinosaurus* roamed the Arctic. It lived near the North Pole. The climate there was warmer than it is now. But it still got cold enough to snow sometimes.

Length: 18 to 23 feet (5.5 to 7 m)

Weight: 3.3 to 4.4 tons (3 to 4 metric tons)

Appearance

Pachyrhinosaurus was related to *Triceratops*. It walked on four legs and ate plants. It had a

When Did This Dinosaur Live?

Triassic Period | Jurassic Period | Cretaceous Period

252 million years ago | 201 million years ago | 145 million years ago | 66 million years ago

Pachyrhinosaurus fossil

large frill covered in horns. But it had no horns on its face or nose. Instead, a thick, bony bulge covered this area. *Pachyrhinosaurus* was similar in size to an elephant.

Who Is the Boss?

Pachyrhinosaurus lived in herds. Similar to rhinoceroses today, *Pachyrhinosaurus* males may have shoved or butted each other with their thick noses. They likely did this to show who was in charge.

PARASAUROLOPHUS

(peh-ruh-sohr-AH-luh-fuhs)

Dinosaur's Call

In 1997, scientists played a loud, low trumpeting sound. It was the call of a *Parasaurolophus.* The scientists had used a fossil of its skull and a computer to figure out what it may have sounded like. This hadrosaur was around during the Late Cretaceous Period. It lived in what is now North America.

Length:
39 feet
(12 m)

Weight:
3.3 tons
(3 metric tons)

Appearance

Parasaurolophus could walk on two or four legs. Like other hadrosaurs,

When Did This Dinosaur Live?

Triassic Period | Jurassic Period | Cretaceous Period

252 million years ago | 201 million years ago | 145 million years ago | 66 million years ago

Parasaurolophus fossil

it had a duck-like bill. This dinosaur grew as long as a school bus.

Trombone Head

Parasaurolophus had a long, hollow bone on its head. Its shape was similar to the curved tubes of a trombone. The dinosaur sent air from its nose through the bone. The air caused the bone to vibrate and make sounds. This was similar to how a person can make music by blowing into a trombone. The air travels through the trombone's tubes and vibrates to make sound.

PLATEOSAURUS

(PLAT-ee-uh-SOHR-uhs)

Range

Dozens of *Plateosaurus* skeletons have been found all over Europe. These dinosaurs were one of the most common plant-eaters in this area during the Late Triassic Period. At this time, dinosaurs had just begun to evolve.

Length:
23 to 26 feet
(7 to 8 m)

Weight:
4.4 tons
(4 metric tons)

Appearance

Plateosaurus was one of the first dinosaurs to grow to a large size. It was a bit bigger than an elephant. It had a long neck with a small head. It could walk on four legs or rise up on its back legs. That let it eat from the tops of tall plants.

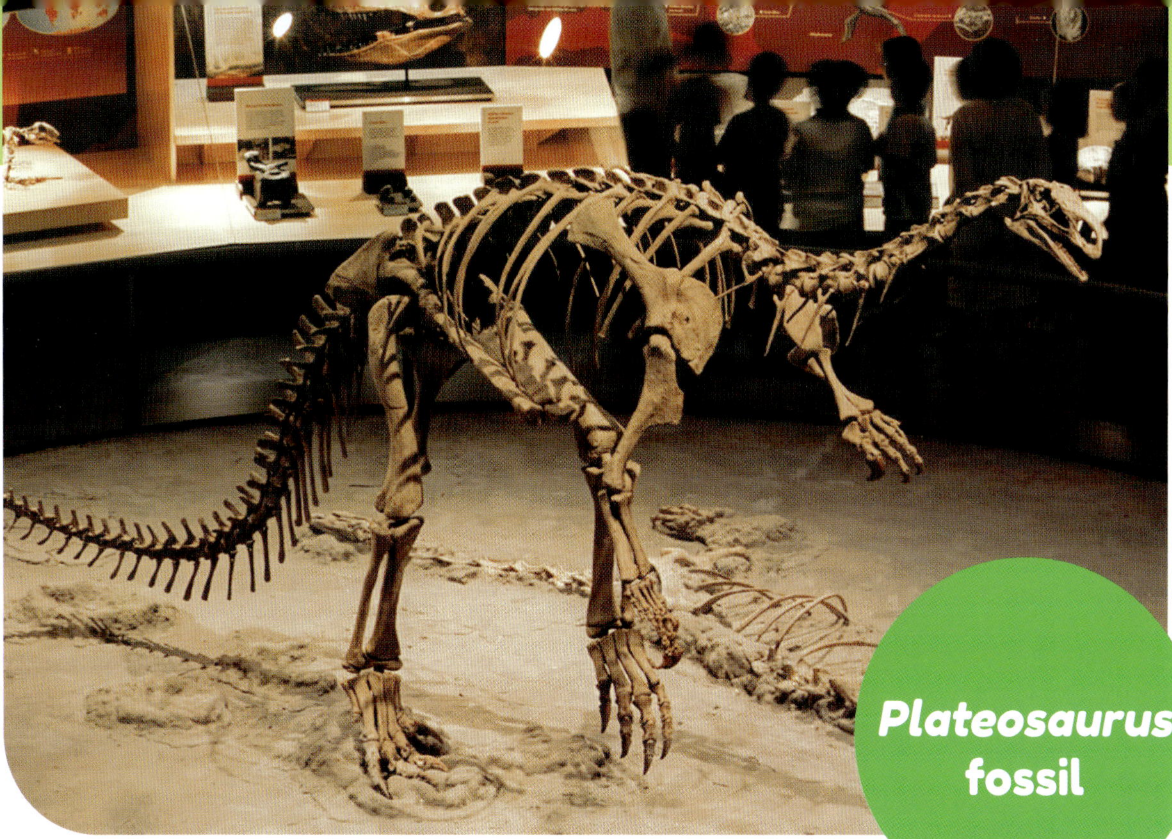

Plateosaurus fossil

Destined for Greatness

Over millions of years, *Plateosaurus* and its relatives evolved. They got bigger and bigger. Their descendants are the huge sauropods and titanosaurs.

When Did This Dinosaur Live?

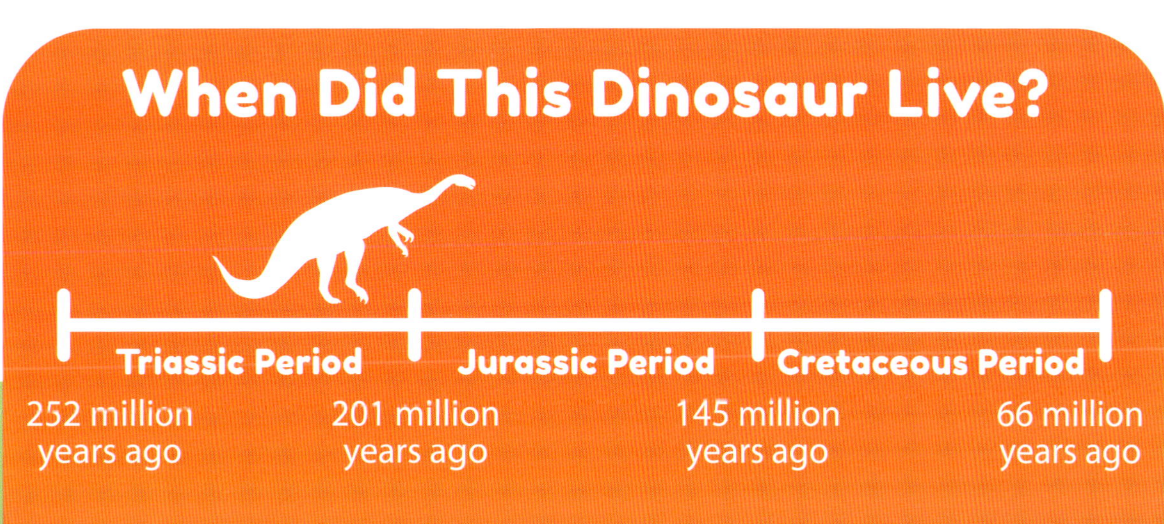

SINOSAUROPTERYX

(SEYE-noh-sohr-AHP-ter-ihks)

Feathered Dinosaur

The first *Sinosauropteryx* fossil stunned scientists. Marks of feathers surrounded the body. Farmers discovered the fossil in China in 1996. It was the first feathered dinosaur ever found. Now scientists know that many dinosaurs had feathers. *Sinosauropteryx* lived during the Early Cretaceous Period.

Length:
3.3 feet
(1 m)

Weight:
6.6 pounds
(3 kg)

Appearance

Sinosauropteryx was small. It was also fast. The dinosaur had long rear legs, short arms, and a

When Did This Dinosaur Live?

Triassic Period | Jurassic Period | Cretaceous Period

252 million years ago
201 million years ago
145 million years ago
66 million years ago

long tail. It was similar in size to a goose. Scientists have even figured out some of *Sinosauropteryx*'s colors. It was reddish brown with light-colored stripes running down its tail.

Sinosauropteryx fossil

Why Feathers?

Sinosauropteryx could not fly. Its feathers were very short. Perhaps the feathers kept it warm. Or maybe the colors helped the dinosaur hide. *Sinosauropteryx* hunted small animals.

SPINOSAURUS

(spine-oh-SOHR-uhs)

Range

Spinosaurus lived during the Late Cretaceous Period. It hunted in rivers in what is now northern Africa. Fossils have been found in Egypt and Morocco.

Length:
50 feet
(15 m)

Weight:
7 tons
(6.4 metric tons)

Appearance

Spinosaurus had a ridge on its back called a sail. The sail could be 6 feet (1.8 m) tall. Sharp teeth filled its long, crocodile-like snout. This huge predator mostly ate fish. *Spinosaurus* weighed

When Did This Dinosaur Live?

Triassic Period	Jurassic Period	Cretaceous Period	
252 million years ago	201 million years ago	145 million years ago	66 million years ago

Spinosaurus fossil

about the same as a school bus. But it grew much longer. It is the largest meat-eating dinosaur ever found. It was 10 feet (3 m) longer than *Tyrannosaurus*.

Super Swimmer

In 2020, scientists found a *Spinosaurus* tail fossil for the first time. The tail was flat. This meant the dinosaur spent most of its life in the water. It was the first swimming dinosaur ever discovered.

STEGOSAURUS

(STEHG-uh-SOHR-uhs)

Range

Stegosaurus is one of the most well-known dinosaurs. It lived during the Late Jurassic Period. It roamed what is now the United States. It grazed on low-growing plants such as ferns.

Appearance

Two rows of tall plates ran down *Stegosaurus*'s back. Its tail ended in a group of spikes. Some scientists call this spiky weapon a thagomizer.

Stegosaurus fossil

This dinosaur grew larger than an elephant. Its brain was very small for its size.

Mysterious Plates

Many people wonder what *Stegosaurus*'s tall plates were for. They were too fragile to work as armor. They may have been for display. Most scientists think they could take in heat in sunlight and release heat in shade. This means they could help *Stegosaurus* control its body temperature.

Length:
29 feet
(9 m)

Weight:
3.3 tons
(3 metric tons)

STYRACOSAURUS

(steye-RAK-uh-SOHR-uhs)

Range

Styracosaurus fossils come from the northern United States and Canada. These plant-eaters lived during the Late Cretaceous Period. They traveled in herds.

Appearance

Styracosaurus was a ceratopsian with style. Its nose horn grew up to 2 feet (0.6 m) long. Six more horns

Length:
18 feet
(5.5 m)

Weight:
3.3 tons
(3 metric tons)

When Did This Dinosaur Live?

Triassic Period	Jurassic Period	Cretaceous Period	
252 million years ago	201 million years ago	145 million years ago	66 million years ago

stuck out from the top of a frill on the back of its head. Bony nubs lined the sides of the frill. *Styracosaurus* was around the same size as a small elephant. Like its cousin *Triceratops*, it had a beak-like mouth and walked on four legs.

***Styracosaurus* skull**

No Grass to Graze On

Most grasses did not appear until after dinosaurs had died out. *Styracosaurus* and other grazers likely fed on shrubs. Those included ferns, palms, and other similar plants.

SUCHOMIMUS

(soo-koh-MEYE-muhs)

Range

Suchomimus fossils were found in the Sahara Desert. This creature lived during the Cretaceous Period. At that time, the area was swampy and dangerous. It was filled with rivers and deadly dinosaurs.

Appearance

The name *Suchomimus* means "crocodile mimic." The jaws of this large predator looked like those of a crocodile. It had around 100 teeth that curved backward. But this dinosaur was more than twice the size of a crocodile. It moved around on two powerful back legs. Spikes ran down its back. These may have supported a sail.

Length:
36 feet
(11 m)

Weight:
2.2 tons
(2 metric tons)

Suchomimus fossil

River Hunter

Suchomimus likely hunted fish and other animals. It had very large, sharp, curved claws on its thumbs. It may have used these claws to spear fish.

When Did This Dinosaur Live?

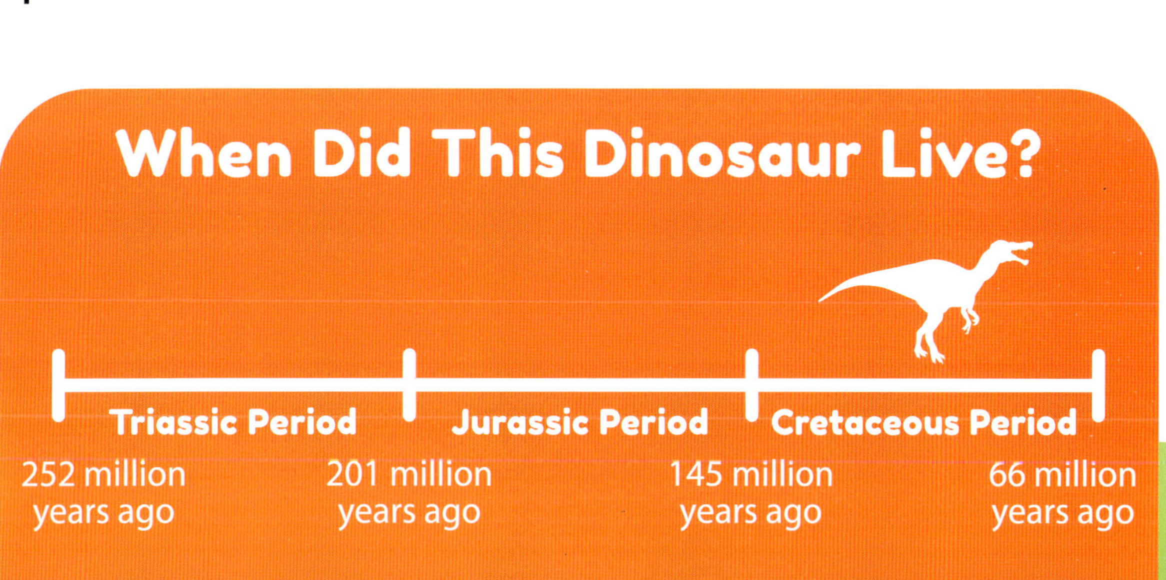

TARBOSAURUS

(TAHR-boh-SOHR-uhs)

Range

Tarbosaurus was the king of dinosaurs in what is now Mongolia. It lived during the Late Cretaceous Period. *Tarbosaurus* was a close cousin of *Tyrannosaurus*.

Appearance

Tarbosaurus had powerful back legs. It also had very short arms. This dinosaur ran on two legs. It held out its thick tail for balance. It had a large head and very sharp teeth. Some scientists think *Tarbosaurus* should be considered a type of *Tyrannosaurus*. Others think it is different enough to have its own name.

Length:
33 feet
(10 m)

Weight:
4.4 tons
(4 metric tons)

Tarbosaurus fossil

Stolen Skeleton

In 2012, a company in the United States sold a *Tarbosaurus* skeleton for $1 million. Then the government of Mongolia showed that the fossil had been stolen from its country. The sale was canceled. The fossil was returned to Mongolia.

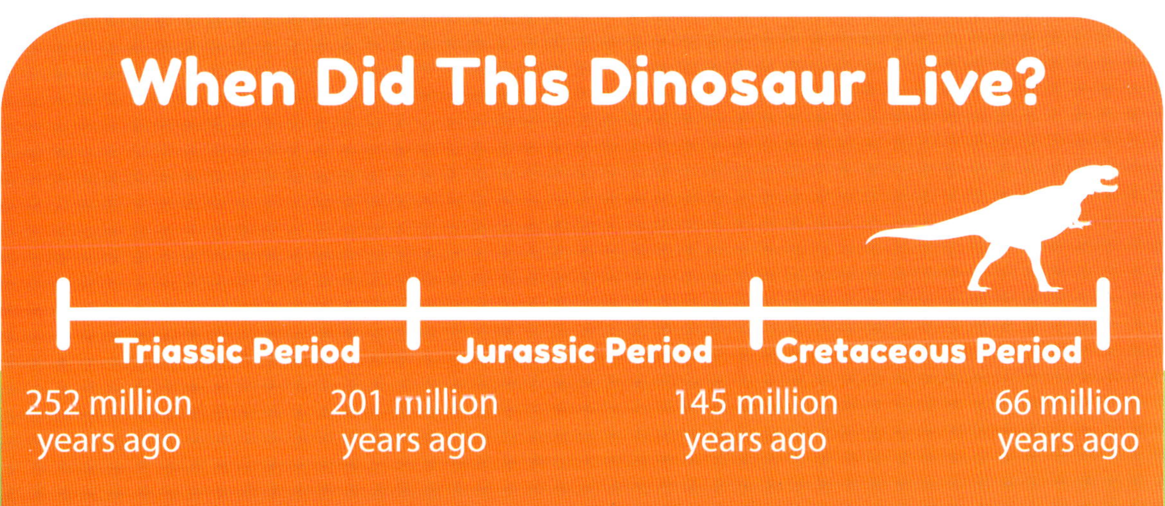

THERIZINOSAURUS

(THEHR-ih-zee-nuh-SOHR-uhs)

Range

Therizinosaurus was a large dinosaur. It was around during the Late Cretaceous Period. It lived in what is now Asia.

Appearance

Therizinosaurus had the longest claws of any known dinosaur. These sword-like talons grew up to 3 feet (0.9 m) long. *Therizinosaurus's* arms were very long too. The dinosaur walked on two strong back legs. It had a round belly, a long neck, and a small beak for a mouth. It had a long tail. Scientists think this dinosaur was probably covered in feathers.

Length:
33 feet
(10 m)

Weight:
1 to 5 tons
(0.9 to 4.5 metric tons)

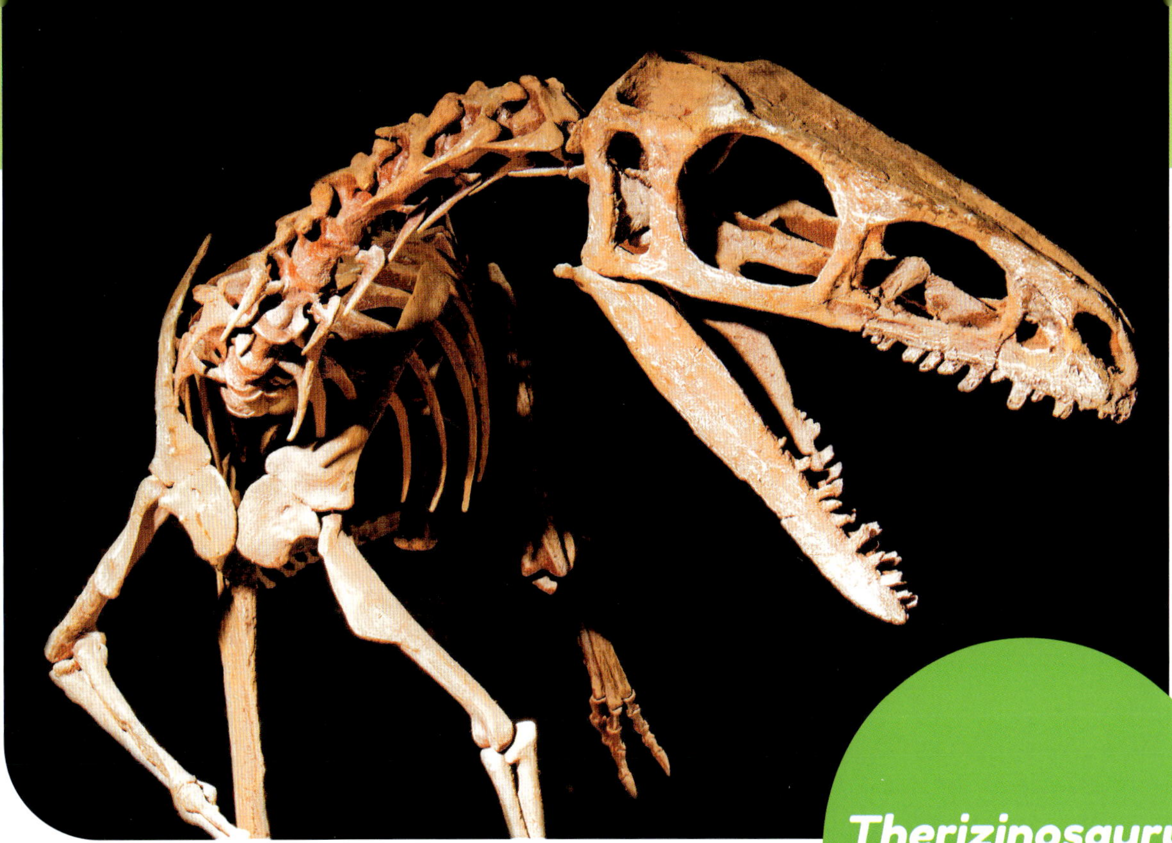

Therizinosaurus fossil

Eat Those Veggies

Therizinosaurus most likely ate plants. It may have used its long claws as rakes to gather vegetation. Some people think it used its claws to fight off predators.

When Did This Dinosaur Live?

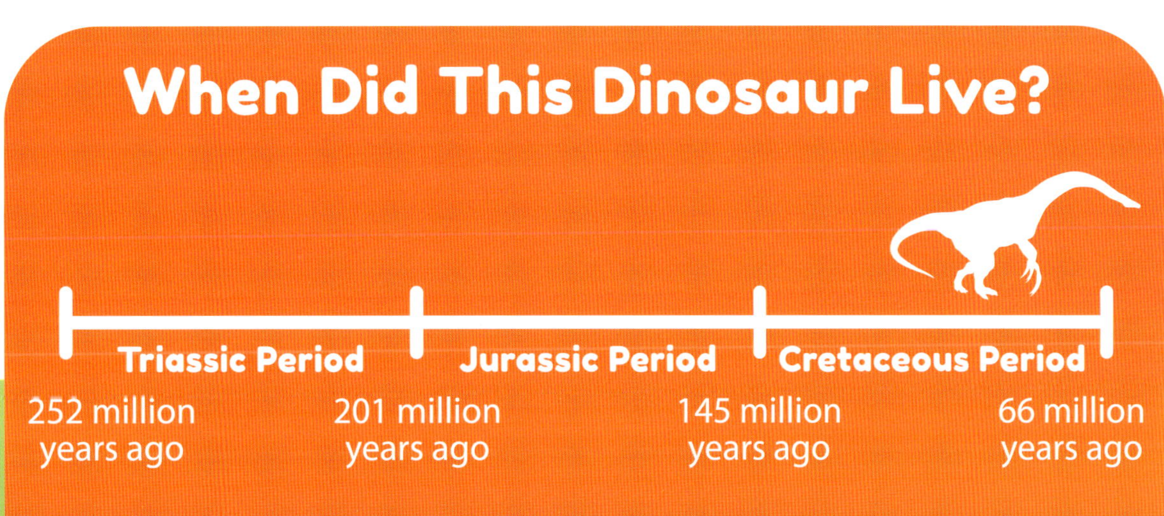

TRICERATOPS

(treye-SEH-ruh-tahps)

Range

Triceratops was one of the most common dinosaurs in what is now North America. It lived during the Late Cretaceous Period. Then a large asteroid struck Earth. That event wiped out *Triceratops* and all the other large dinosaurs.

Appearance

The name *Triceratops* means "three-horned face." This dinosaur had two horns over its eyes. A third horn was on its nose. It also had a wide, flat frill.

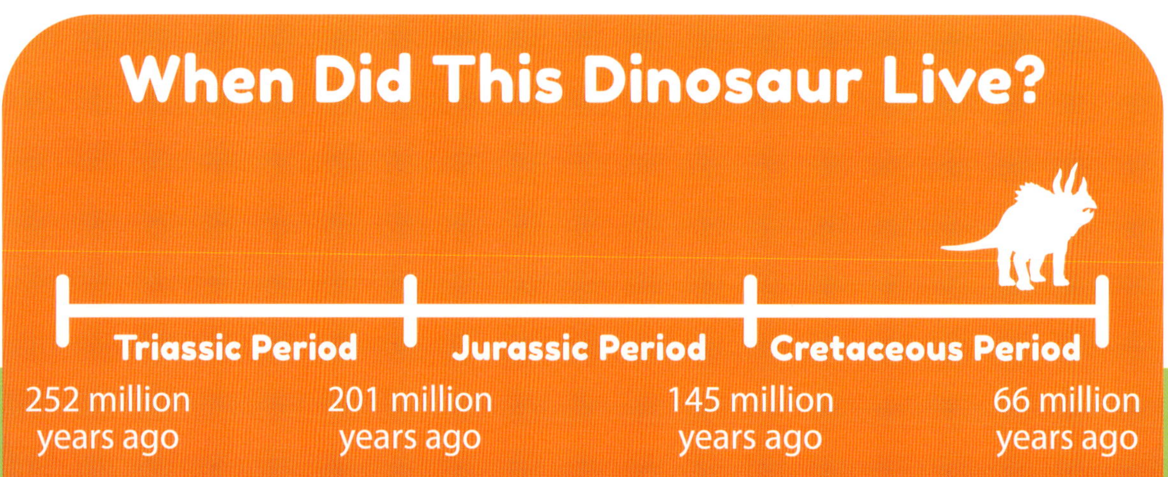

Triceratops fossil

Triceratops was around the same size as a large elephant. It grazed on plants. It had a hooked, toothless beak.

Battling the King

People have wondered if *Triceratops* ever had to deal with attacks from the mighty *Tyrannosaurus*. One fossil has bones from both dinosaurs. Scientists are studying it to find out if these two dinosaurs died fighting each other.

Length:
30 feet
(9 m)

Weight:
8.8 tons
(8 metric tons)

TROODON

(TROH-oh-dahn)

Range

Scientists think *Troodon* was probably one of the smartest dinosaurs. It was small for a dinosaur. But it had a very large brain. It lived in the northern parts of what is now North America. It was around during the Late Cretaceous Period.

Appearance

Troodon most likely had feathers. It was very light. *Troodon* ran quickly on its two back legs. It likely ate small animals that it grabbed with its strong arms.

Length:
6.6 feet
(2 m)

Weight:
55 pounds
(25 kg)

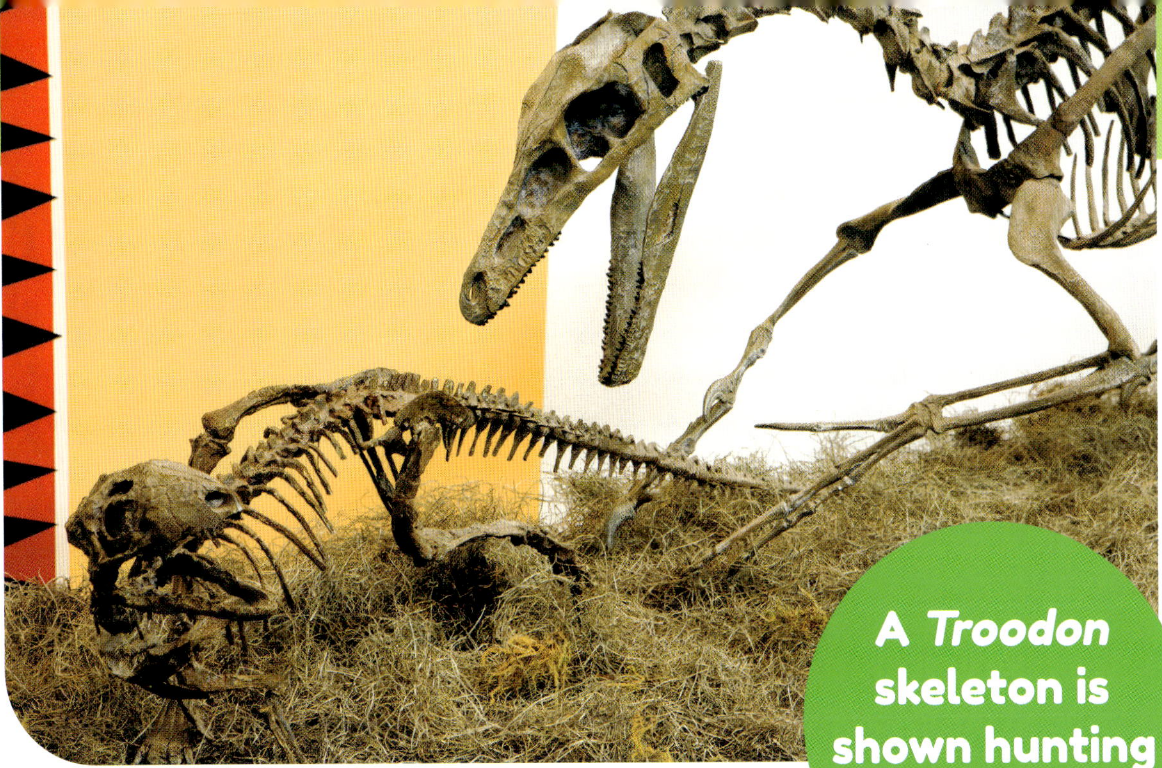

A *Troodon* skeleton is shown hunting *Orodromeus.*

Night Vision

Troodon lived so far north that the sun would not rise at all for part of the year. Its large eyes made it possible to hunt in the dark. Troodon laid eggs in nests on the ground. One or both parents likely guarded the nest.

When Did This Dinosaur Live?

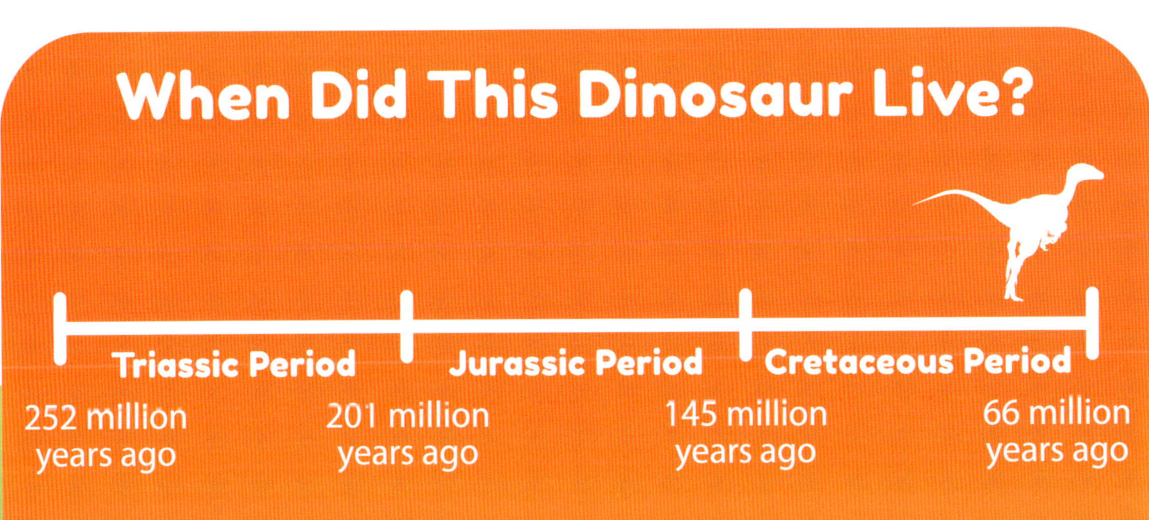

TYRANNOSAURUS

(teye-RAN-uh-SOHR-uhs)

Dinosaur King

Tyrannosaurus rex is probably the most famous dinosaur. Its name means "king of the tyrant lizards." It was one species of a type of dinosaur called *Tyrannosaurus*. It roamed what is now North America. It lived during the Cretaceous Period.

Length:
40 feet
(12 m)

Weight:
6.6 tons
(6 metric tons)

Appearance

Despite its name, *Tyrannosaurus* was not the biggest dinosaur.

When Did This Dinosaur Live?

Triassic Period	Jurassic Period	Cretaceous Period	
252 million years ago	201 million years ago	145 million years ago	66 million years ago

Sue is the largest *Tyrannosaurus rex* fossil ever discovered.

But it was still huge. This meat-eater was around the same size as a school bus. It ran quickly on two powerful back legs. It had tiny, two-fingered arms. Its teeth were as long as bananas. Its bite was strong enough to crush a car. *Tyrannosaurus* most likely had feathers.

Meet Sue

The Field Museum is in Chicago. It has a *Tyrannosaurus* fossil. A fossil hunter named Susan Hendrickson found it. The fossil is named "Sue" after her.

UTAHRAPTOR

(YOO-tah-rap-ter)

Range

Utahraptor is named after the state of Utah. This is where scientists first found its fossils. *Utahraptor* lived in this area during the Early Cretaceous Period. *Utahraptor* was part of a group of dinosaurs called raptors. *Utahraptor* was the largest of the raptors. Raptors evolved to become smaller over time. Eventually, they became birds.

Length:
20 feet
(6 m)

Weight:

1.1 tons
(1 metric ton)

Appearance

Utahraptor was built to kill. It had sharp claws on its three fingers. Its mouth was filled with knife-like teeth. Each claw was about the size of a human thumb. *Utahraptor* was likely covered in feathers.

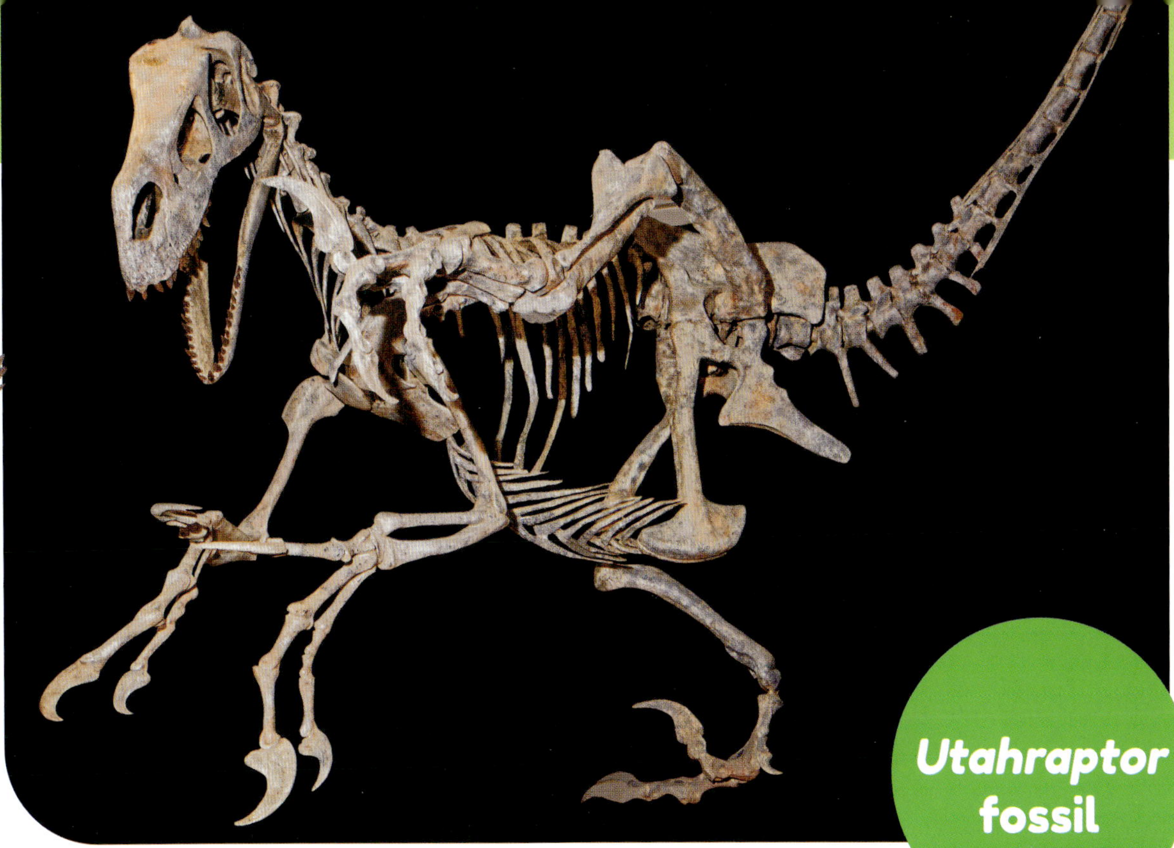

Utahraptor fossil

Dangerous Feet

Utahraptor hunted and ate other animals. It likely stabbed prey with its feet. A curved talon came out from the middle toe of each foot. This talon was 15 inches (38 cm) long.

When Did This Dinosaur Live?

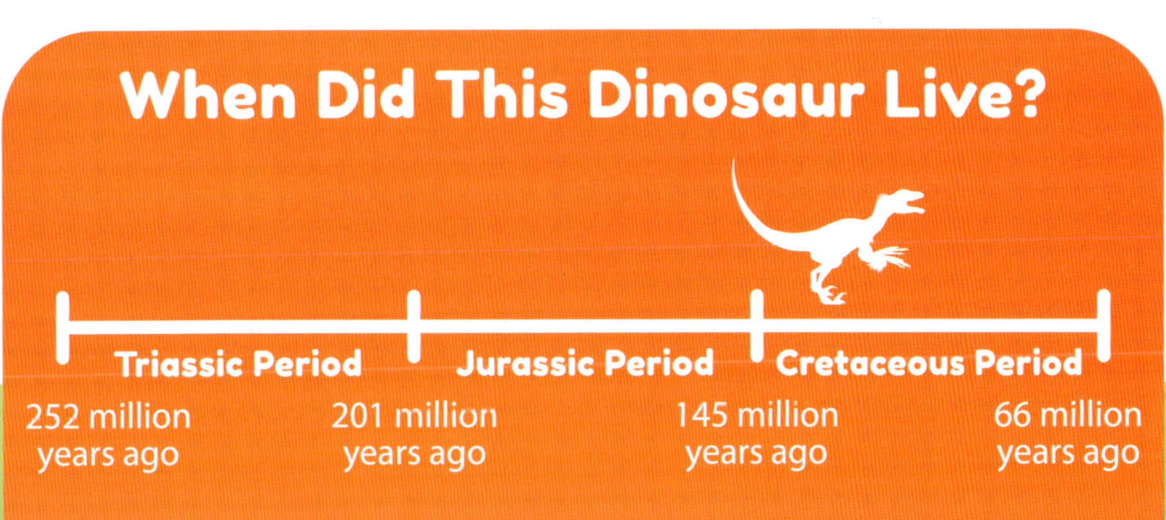

VELOCIRAPTOR

(veh-LAH-sih-rap-ter)

Range

Velociraptor hunted in what is now Mongolia. It was alive during the Late Cretaceous Period. This dinosaur stars in the *Jurassic Park* movies. However, the movies do not show what it was really like. The movies' dinosaurs were inspired by another raptor called *Deinonychus*.

Length:
6 feet
(1.8 m)

Weight:
66 pounds
(30 kg)

Appearance

Velociraptor was small. It was around the size of a turkey. It was covered in feathers. It had a very long tail. It likely used this for balance while running. Like other raptors, it was a meat-eater. It could stab prey with large claws on its feet.

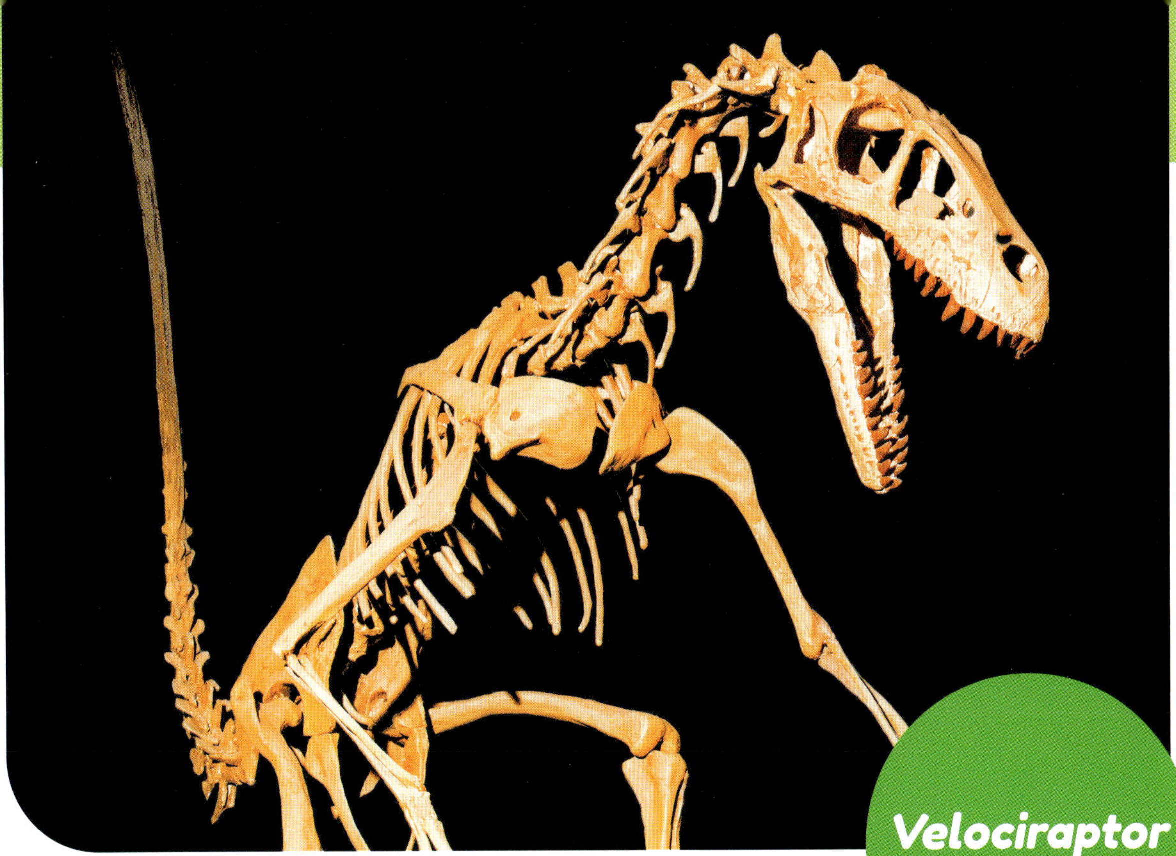

Velociraptor fossil

Warm Feathers

Velociraptor could not fly. Its feathers likely kept it warm. They may have also helped the dinosaur warm its eggs while sitting on its nest.

When Did This Dinosaur Live?

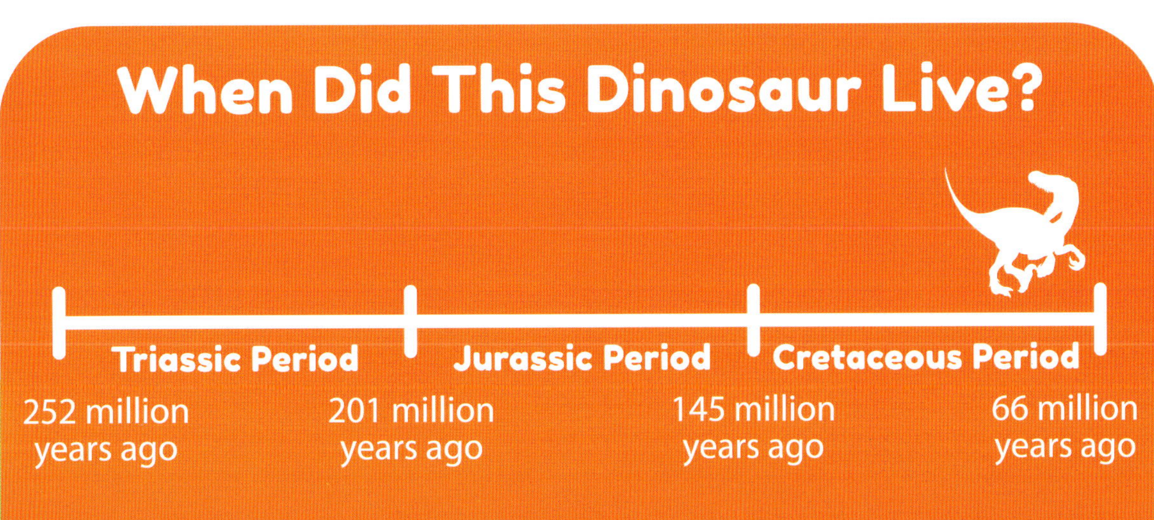

GLOSSARY

climate
The typical weather conditions of an area.

crest
A feature on the top of an animal's head.

descendants
Creatures that evolved from animals that lived at an earlier time.

display
In nature, when an animal uses a body feature to attract or threaten others.

evolve
To change slowly over many generations.

fragile
Delicate and not very strong.

frill
A flat area extending from an animal's neck or head.

mimic
Something that looks like another thing.

predator
An animal that hunts and eats other animals.

preserved
Saved in good condition over time.

prey
An animal that is hunted by other animals.

serrated
Jagged along the edges, like a saw.

species
A group of living things that are all similar enough to mate with each other.

venom
A toxic material made by animals such as snakes. Venomous animals bite or sting to inject venom, which can cause pain or death.

TO LEARN MORE

More Books to Read

Blasing, George, and Cary Woodruff. *Dinosaur Encyclopedia for Kids: The Big Book of Prehistoric Creatures*. Rockridge, 2022.

Murray, Julie. *Tyrannosaurus Rex*. Abdo, 2020.

Online Resources

To learn more about dinosaurs, please visit **abdobooklinks.com** or scan this QR code. These links are routinely monitored and updated to provide the most current information available.

PHOTO CREDITS

Cover Photos: Shutterstock, front (*Tyrannosaurus*), front (*Stegosaurus*); Daniel Eskridge/Shutterstock, front (*Apatosaurus*); Free Video Photo Agency/Shutterstock, front (desert landscape); Herschel Hoffmeyer/Shutterstock, front (*Triceratops*), back

Interior Photos: Herschel Hoffmeyer/Shutterstock, 1, 6–7, 16–17, 28–29, 104–105, 106–107, 114–115, 118–119, 120 (top); Shutterstock, 3, 5 (top), 5 (bottom), 7 (bottom) 8 (bottom), 8–9, 12 (bottom), 14 (bottom), 14–15, 16 (bottom), 19 (bottom), 21 (bottom), 22 (bottom), 24, 25 (bottom), 27 (bottom), 29 (bottom), 30 (bottom), 32 (bottom), 34, 35 (top), 35 (bottom), 38–39, 40 (top), 42–43, 43 (bottom), 44–45, 45 (bottom), 46–47, 47 (bottom), 48 (bottom), 50–51, 51, 52 (bottom), 52–53, 54–55, 55 (bottom), 56–57, 62, 64–65, 65 (bottom), 66 (bottom), 68 (bottom), 68–69, 70–71, 71 (bottom), 74–75, 75 (bottom), 76 (top), 78–79, 80 (bottom), 80–81, 82, 83 (bottom), 84–85, 89 (top), 89 (bottom), 90–91, 92, 94 (bottom), 94–95, 98 (bottom), 100, 101 (bottom), 102 (bottom), 108 (top), 108 (bottom), 111 (bottom), 112, 113 (bottom), 121, 122–123, 124–125; Ameli Au/Shutterstock, 4; Millard H. Sharp/Science Source, 7 (top), 25 (top), 31, 43 (top), 65 (top), 73, 77, 85, 109, 115 (top), 123 (top), 125 (top); Francois Gohier/Science Source, 9, 13, 15, 45 (top), 117; Julius T. Csotonyi/Science Source, 10–11; Martin Shields/Science Source, 11 (top); Morph Art Creation/Shutterstock, 11 (bottom), 86 (bottom); YuRi Photolife/Shutterstock, 12–13, 20–21, 22 (top), 36–37, 86 (top); Dorling Kindersley/Science Source, 17, 18–19; Carlos Goldin/Science Source, 19 (top); The Natural History Museum, London/Science Source, 21 (top), 33, 41, 47 (top), 53, 55 (top), 66–67, 81, 83 (top); Eric Nathan/Alamy, 23; Arthur Dorety/Stocktrek Images/Science Source, 26; Akkharat Jarusilawong/Shutterstock, 27 (top), 95; Johnnie Rik/Shutterstock, 29 (top); Daniel Eskridge/Shutterstock, 30–31, 61 (top), 96–97, 98–99; Rodos Studio Ferhat Cinar/Shutterstock, 32 (top); Irina Shemshura/Shutterstock, 36 (bottom), 38 (bottom), 50 (bottom), 56 (bottom), 58 (bottom), 61 (bottom), 63 (bottom), 76 (bottom), 78 (bottom), 84 (bottom), 93 (bottom), 104 (bottom), 106 (bottom), 115 (bottom), 116 (bottom), 119 (bottom), 120 (bottom), 123 (bottom), 125 (bottom); Dani Pozo/AFP/Getty Images, 37; Kazuhiro Nogi/AFP/Getty Images, 39; Nora Hachio/Shutterstock, 40 (bottom), 91 (bottom); Nobumichi Tamura/Stocktrek Images/Getty Images, 48–49, 72 (bottom), 72–73; Jacqueline Larma/AP Images, 49; Lisa Maree Williams/Getty Images News/Getty Images, 57; Chastity Q./Shutterstock, 58–59; Frederic J. Brown/AFP/Getty Images, 59; Henry H. Herrmann/Ullstein Bild Dtl./Getty Images, 60; New York Public Library/Science Source, 63 (top); Porco Rosso/Shutterstock, 67; Mike Kemp/In Pictures/Getty Images, 69; Faviel Raven/Shutterstock, 71 (top); Kevin Schafer/The Image Bank/Getty Images, 75 (top); Conchi Martinez/Shutterstock, 79; William West/AFP/Getty Images, 87; DK Images/Science Source, 88–89; Bill O'Leary/The Washington Post/Getty Images, 91 (top); Danny Ye/Shutterstock, 93 (top); Florian Augustin/Shutterstock, 96 (bottom); Stephen J. Krasemann/Science Source, 97; Pao W./Shutterstock, 99; Xavi Gomez/Cover/Getty Images, 101 (top); Masato Hattori/Science Source, 102–103; Bernard Weil/Toronto Star/Getty Images, 103; Josep Lago/AFP/Getty Images, 105; Paul Barron/Shutterstock, 107; Martin Weber/Shutterstock, 110–111; Vanderlei Almeida/AFP/Getty Images, 111 (top); Marco Ansaloni/Science Source, 113 (top); Freestyle Images/Shutterstock, 116 (top); Craig Larcom/Alamy, 119 (top)